Psychics

Psychics

**by the editors
of *Psychic* Magazine**

Harper & Row,
Publishers

New York
Evanston
San Francisco
London

All photographs were taken by John Larsen, San Francisco, with the exception of the photograph of Douglas Johnson taken by Malcolm Bessent. The pictures are used by permission of *Psychic Magazine,* 680 Beach Street, San Francisco, California 94109.

PSYCHICS. Copyright © 1972 by The Bolen Company. All rights reserved. Printed in the United States of America. No part of this book may be used or reproduced in any manner whatsoever without written permission except in the case of brief quotations embodied in critical articles and reviews. For information address Harper & Row, Publishers, Inc., 49 East 33rd Street, New York, N.Y. 10016. Published simultaneously in Canada by Fitzhenry & Whiteside Limited, Toronto.

FIRST EDITION

LIBRARY OF CONGRESS CATALOG CARD NUMBER: 72-183641

Contents

Preface *by Alan Vaughan*	vii
Jeane Dixon	1
Arthur Ford	15
Eileen J. Garrett	31
Irene F. Hughes	47
Peter Hurkos	65
Douglas Johnson	79
Kreskin	95
Sybil Leek	113
James A. Pike	131

Preface

by Alan Vaughan

Psychic Magazine was established in 1969 in San Francisco by James Grayson Bolen to explore "the core part of human nature and the mysteries of the universe" in a way that the sophisticated layman could understand. Each issue features an interview with psychics, scientists, and others who have devoted their lives to experiment and experience of psychic phenomena. In addition to Mr. Bolen's interviews, I have had the privilege of countributing dialogues with Arthur Ford, Irene Hughes, and Douglas Johnson to this volume.

To find a comparable format, one must look to the dialogues of Plato or to the gospels of the Bible, in which Jesus was questioned about the strange phenomena we term "psychic." The word *psyche*, Greek for "soul," has as its symbol the dove, which in turn symbolizes other life-giving concepts, such as Love and Peace.

But by whatever symbol, the core part of human nature provides the reality from which proceed psychic ways of knowing and understanding one another. To our common-sense logic, rooted in our narrow experience of things we can touch, see, and measure, psychic phenomena are "impossible" because they cannot be "explained." Yet early man accepted these phenomena as a manifestation of a divinity greater than himself, and celebrated his participation in that divinity with rituals of life, death, and rebirth.

Technological civilizations of the West have cut man off from that heritage, but now the seeds of his innate spirituality are beginning to sprout from the cracks of concrete science to promise a new age of rebirth and growth. More and more scientists as well as intelligent laymen are beginning to question the life-denying principles of materialism as scientists probe deeper into the heart of the atom and look to the core of the universe where they find phenomena becoming as "impossible" as those of the psyche. The present flirtation of Science with Religion may become a marriage bond if it is found that their mysteries spring from a single Source.

Early in life, I learned two helpful rules in doing research: (1) ask somebody who knows; (2) always go to the top. Mr. Bolen graduated from the same school of life, and so the interviews presented here are with some of the top psychics in the world. For Arthur Ford and Eileen Garrett, whose fame developed in an earlier generation, their interviews were the last they gave. It was also the last such interview for Bishop James Pike, who died in the Judean desert in his search for Christ.

Almost singlehandedly Bishop Pike turned the nation's and the world's thoughts to the possibility of life after death as a reality—and sparked a renewed interest in the basic principles and origins of religion. That interest is now broadening and becoming more sophisticated. Just how meaningful it becomes may depend on how well we are able to comprehend its significance and utilize its promise in our daily lives. The personalities interviewed here show by their own lives and philosophies that the treasures of the soul need not be hoarded "for heaven," but can become the very coinage of life.

Their message to the world has been said many times and many ways. Paul said it to Timothy two millennia ago:

"Neglect not the gift that is in thee, which was given thee by prophecy. . . ."

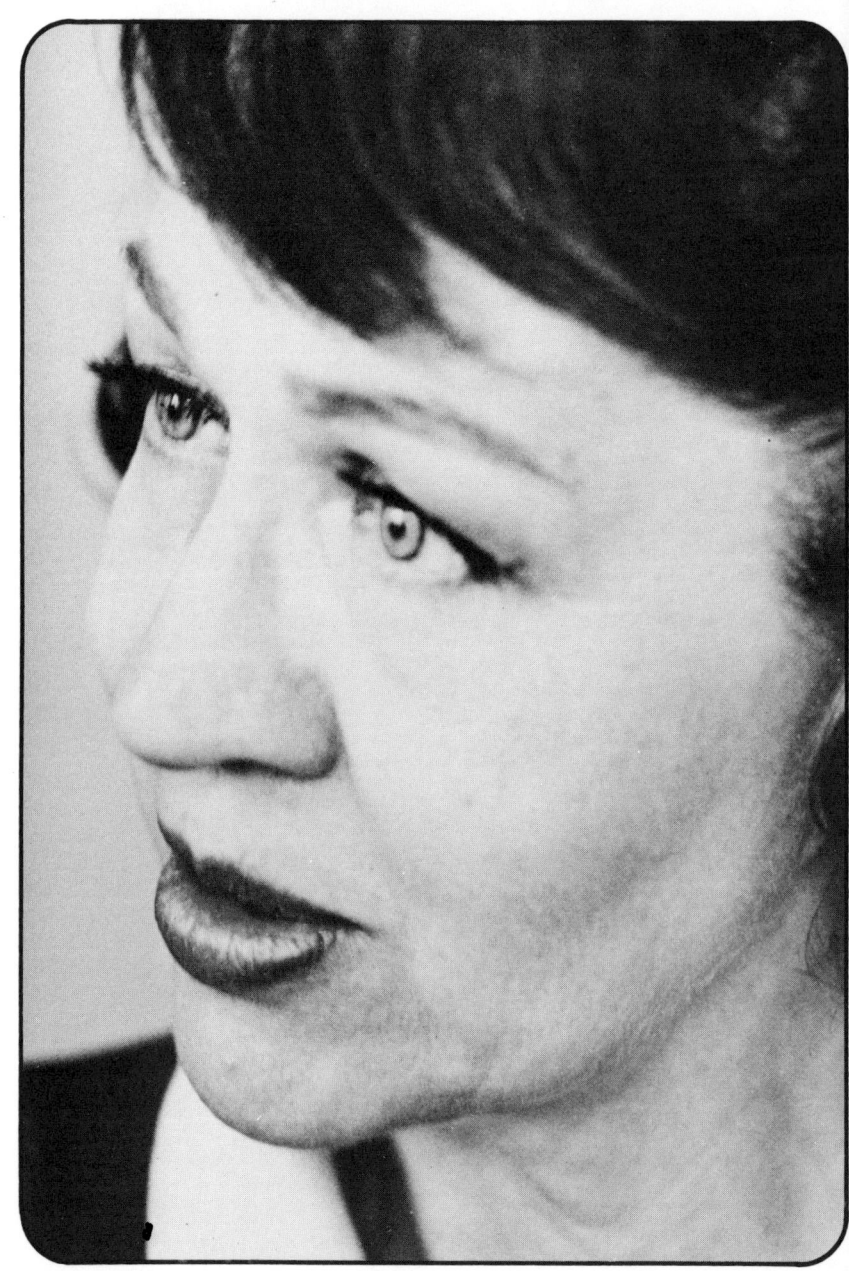

one
Jeane Dixon

Jeane Dixon was born in a small Wisconsin lumber town just before the armistice was signed ending World War I.

Her parents, Frank and Emma Pinckert, who had immigrated to this country from Germany several years before, moved the family to California shortly after their daughter's birth.

It was as a young girl in Santa Rosa, then a small provincial community fifty miles north of San Francisco, that Jeane Dixon began to tell about events which subsequently occurred.

Once she asked her mother for a letter edged in black, which came a few days later informing the family of a grandfather's death in Germany. Another time she talked about the black-and-white puppy her father bought while on a business trip in Chicago, which he later brought home as a surprise.

It was also in Santa Rosa during her formative years that an old Gypsy woman told the Pinckerts their daughter had the gift of prophecy. The Gypsy based her reading on lines in the child's palms—notably a Star of David in the left one and a star which reaches out in all directions in the right.

Later a Jesuit priest, learned in palmistry as well as astrology, supported the Gypsy's reading. He also added to it by predicting that one day the young girl would be famous.

From Santa Rosa, the Pinckerts moved to Los Angeles where the family home was permanently established. Despite new surroundings, the young clairvoyante continued to talk about her glimpses of the future.

After completing high school in Los Angeles, she pursued a stage career until her marriage to James Dixon. Mrs. Dixon then gave up her theatrical pursuits to become a full-time housewife. Dixon, an old friend of the family, was a partner with movie producer Hal Roach in a Los Angeles automobile agency at the time.

Following the outbreak of World War II, however, he became a dollar-a-year man for the federal government. Because of his wartime duties and the distance from Los Angeles to the nation's capital, the Dixons moved to Washington, D.C. They have lived there ever since.

Professionally, Jeane Dixon is a real estate broker in her husband's firm, James L. Dixon & Company, which handles residential properties and specializes in finding facilities for foreign embassies in Washington. She inadvertently became involved in the property field when her husband insisted she use him and his office as a shield against the many requests that began pouring in as her popularity as a seeress grew.

A devout Catholic who attends mass daily, Jeane Dixon meditates and prays routinely and never hesitates to talk about God, His work, and her own beliefs and practices. Her psychic ability, she believes, is a God-given talent that is to be used to help and benefit others.

Today the psychic side of her life is spent lecturing, writing, and predicting. This includes traditionally releasing annual predictions to the media each New Year's day for the year ahead, making prophetic comments throughout the year, and writing a nationally syndicated astrology column. In addition, she has been the subject of a best seller, A Gift of Prophecy, *the story of her life. The book was first published in 1965 and has gone through over eighteen printings.*

Jeane Dixon's activities also extend to social and philanthropic projects. As an outgrowth of this, she founded a multi-million-dollar nonprofit organization called Children to Children, dedicated to helping youngsters throughout the world. The Foundation will sponsor and foster cultural exchanges in education, arts, crafts, and the sciences through the latest technology, as well as cooperate with all civic and governmental organizations, to promote spiritual, mental, and physical growth of children.

James and Jeane Dixon live in a four-story colonial-style townhouse within walking distance of their office. Over the years the Seeress of Washington, as she is often called, and her husband have become familiar figures in Washington.

PSYCHIC: Your working profession is real estate, isn't it?
DIXON: Yes, that's my business of living.
PSYCHIC: Do the demands of your psychic talent interfere with your personal, professional, and social life?
DIXON: I suppose I can best answer that by saying if I were a hundred, perhaps even a thousand, people, I don't think I could meet the many demands and requests. I get over three thousand letters each week, and I have one person alone who just opens the mail. Then we must return any money or presents received, because I never accept them; I couldn't. You see, my gift is not for sale. And it seems that not a day goes by but what we don't receive a request for information about a missing person.

I wish I could help everyone, but there just isn't enough time or enough of me. I do the best I can under the circumstances, though. So, you see, this talent of mine is very costly, in more ways than one.

PSYCHIC: Do you ever make use of your sixth sense in your profession?

DIXON: I make use of it every moment of my life. And I think the Lord has given all of us extrasensory perception and we are meant to use it.

For example, I can feel the positive feeling a house might have for people. When it's negative, I tell them, but if they insist on buying it, that's their decision. If I get a positive feeling, and even if they dislike the house, I'll ask them to buy it—when I know they won't lose any money—if only to try it out for a while.

PSYCHIC: You have often been referred to as a prophet, a psychic, and even an astrologer, though more popularly as the Seeress of Washington. How would you refer to yourself?

DIXON: First, remember that other people have given those "labels" to me—I haven't. I'm just plain Jeane Dixon, trying to do the Lord's will as I feel it upon this earth.

PSYCHIC: Most people have, no doubt, read several popular descriptions of your unusual talent. Perhaps you can describe it in your own words.

DIXON: Well, to me it isn't unusual at all, but I think my husband explained it best as described in *A Gift of Prophecy*. He was once asked, "Isn't it unusual that Jeane predicts these things and they come true?" And he replied, "No, it would be unusual if she didn't."

This happened several years back when I was on television with Ambassador Davies and several others. I told everyone that I got that Malenkov, then in power, would bow out to Bulganin and then would come Khrushchev and that there would be a silver ball launched into space . . . the very first satellite. Everyone laughed, but what I saw did come to pass. So, you see, as my husband explained, it's the usual thing. But I can't get everything, I couldn't possibly.

PSYCHIC: What are your feelings about this talent; how it functions, and where it comes from?.

DIXON: I believe our Lord brings warnings at certain times to let the world know that there is a power greater than ours. And perhaps because of my faith, He gives me these visions, these revelations. Now He could take this talent away from me in two seconds, because He is so almighty and all-powerful. Consequently, I count my blessings every moment.

PSYCHIC: Let's discuss the various facets of your gift, such as telepathy.

DIXON: Telepathy is thought; that is, thought waves. To me this is easy to explain by comparing it to a radio. There are certain channels you turn to get certain stations, correct?

Now we as individuals, all of us, have our own channels right here on earth. And these personal channels lead to one common point, the Holy Trinity—the Father, the Son, and the Holy Spirit, one and the same. So, regardless of our personal channels, we end up in this common point of communication. And no one, incidentally, can have his channel replaced or taken away on earth; it is his alone because the Lord gave it to him. You cannot buy or sell it.

Now, then, if I can tune into your channel—which I cannot always do—I can pick up your thoughts and your vibrations, and your purpose upon this earth. One of the talents I'm grateful for is that I can sometimes tell a person his purpose—why he was born—when I pick up his channel. And this is how I use the crystal ball at times, although it is not necessary, and I should point out it is not just plain glass but mined crystal, a semiprecious stone.

PSYCHIC: How do you use the crystal?

DIXON: Well, I ask the person to concentrate on one thought only and to look into the crystal. The crystal is my point of concentration. And then I try to pick up his channel, which is his point of concentration, because his thoughts are not scattered. His mind is pointed right there in this beautiful crystal and then I can pick up his thoughts. That is telepathy.

PSYCHIC: Is crystal the best substance for this for you or are there similar ones equally good?

DIXON: I don't know because I have never tried anything else except prayer and meditation. Besides, I very rarely use the crystal ball.

PSYCHIC: What about psychometry or touching animate or inanimate objects and being able to "read" information from them through unconventional means?

DIXON: I believe that everything upon this earth has at one time or another been alive. Therefore, there's nothing new, is there? We are just discovering things—everything is as old as time itself; everything has vibrations. You can feel a piece of furniture and almost know how old the wood is in it—by the feel, by your reaction to it.

PSYCHIC: Do you control this or does it just happen?

DIXON: No, I don't control any of this: it's there or it isn't there. Sometimes I can meditate for hours or days and nothing comes. I never like to *force* anything because if I do, then it could be wrong, very wrong. So I like to have things flow in God's timing, in the natural way.

PSYCHIC: What sensations do you experience when you "tip fingers," as you call it?

DIXON: I never know until the moment I touch a person's fingers what will come. It could be what's uppermost on their minds . . . their health, an important thing in their subconscious, or something they are planning. It could even be an event that is going to happen which they are completely unaware of, all the while hovering over them very strongly.

PSYCHIC: Then, you don't tip fingers for certain things—you simply get whatever comes through?

DIXON: Exactly. And I always use this finger [showing the fourth or ring finger, left hand], because for me it's so much more sensitive than the others. I don't get nearly as much from the other fingers, although I do get a great deal just taking hold of the hand.

To get a direct line, though, I use the fourth finger. But don't ask me why; through experience I've found it's the best one.

PSYCHIC: What's your theory on how you are able to do this? How do you think it works?

DIXON: When you ask how it works, that's very difficult. Let me give you an example. If you were to close your eyes and put your finger into a pot of water, you would know several things about it without

actually seeing it. If it was hot, you would pull back quickly, wouldn't you? In a sense, this is how I get information when I touch or tip fingers. And even though my eyes might be closed, I can almost tell a person's height.
PSYCHIC: You get visual impressions?
DIXON: Yes, *great* visual impressions. I receive them as both pictures and symbols, and sometimes I see them in color.
PSYCHIC: Do these impressions include the inner voice you sometimes mention?
DIXON: They could. Whenever I get an inner voice in tipping fingers or getting vibrations, I know the person has great faith, though I can't explain why. Someone who lacks faith has completely different vibrations and the inner voice is different. But these are the things I feel.
PSYCHIC: Are some people easier to "read" for than others?
DIXON: Yes, particularly those from the East. They are much more open, because of their stronger belief in the psychic world, than Westerners. But I never go any further than I think the Lord allows.
PSYCHIC: What about skeptics?
DIXON: I *love* skeptics, because they are so interesting to work with. The more you give, the better life is; so you can give the skeptic a great deal more than you can give someone who already accepts the true spiritual world.

I try hard to help skeptics get in closer contact with the Holy Spirit. I pray and think, if only they would see the light of the Lord within their souls just once . . . they would be so much happier. You see, they close the Almighty out of their lives.
PSYCHIC: To you, then, people have or can set up barriers?
DIXON: Yes, in a way, by not believing. Then it's very difficult to get information.
PSYCHIC: You classify your premonitions into two distinct categories: "sought" predictions and "unsought" predictions, or visions. That is, the psychic or man-willed and the revelationary or God-willed. Would you mind clarifying this?
DIXON: Well, the *sought* includes man's plans and his choices, or telepathy—the psychic worlds.

But the *unsought* are God's plans and come in His timing. They have nothing to do with the psychic world or psychic phenomena, and therefore cannot be known or revealed through seeking. They are visions, revelations. And once you experience one, no one can ever tell you that there is not a greater power in this universe. And the experience . . . well . . . you want to share it with everyone in the world. It's a joy, a peace and freedom all the money in the world can't buy.

As for the revelationary experience itself and the way it happens for me, which I've learned through experience: it begins with three days of preparation, a knowing that something will come. Then on the fourth day the vision—the unsought message—is revealed, followed by three more days of ecstasy, or seven in all. By the eighth day, I'm back to my everyday life, trying to recreate or reach the revelationary experience, thinking I will get it back. And with this, I begin work to free my soul again, but other forces try to take over. I don't know how to say this, but there are good and evil—let's call the "good" our Lord and "evil" the devil . . . there is a balance. But we have to stay on the straight and narrow, in harmony with God's law in the universe. And, oh, how I get upset when I'm misquoted, but I know I must "do unto others as you would be done by." So I forgive and try to forget . . . and, you see, that makes a balance in my life.

PSYCHIC: In regard to the man-willed future, you say that "there is sometimes one tiny little moment in time when you can tip the scales and turn the event aside." You believe this?

DIXON: Where man-made plans are concerned, yes, of course. St. Thomas Aquinas, you know, said that the man-will factor can change because people's minds change, and that's what happens sometimes.

My husband did not take a plane once at my request; he made up his mind at the last second and is here today because of that moment which tipped the scales. The plane crashed.

There is one exception, I might add, and that's destiny . . . the general outline of your life. Destiny leads certain people into definite channels and patterns, and no matter what they do they must conform to the pattern or stay in that channel, because they are men of destiny. Destiny is a definite guide to our purposes.

PSYCHIC: What about your ability to see objective events or things without the use of the five senses, whether past, present, or future? This seems to depend upon more than telepathy. What do you think is the explanation?

DIXON: That is communication through the Holy Trinity—the Father, the Son, and the Holy Spirit. It is from whence we came and to where we return, our point of communication, you see. It is eternal—past, present, future—so it is always there.

PSYCHIC: If you have the ability you can look into it?

DIXON: Yes, but as far as I'm concerned, it's faith that life is eternal and that there is a point of communication.

PSYCHIC: Where did you learn astrology?

DIXON: I learned astrology in California, as a child, from a very wise and consecrated Jesuit priest, Father Henry. He was very interested in my talent and had seen the lines in my hands. It was he who worked my chart. He told me that I was going to hold the hands of some of the great people in the world, and that I would be very famous because God had intended it . . . my destiny. And he added that I would suffer a great deal too, because of misunderstanding. So he thought I should learn astrology and he taught me his system, the old Chaldean method.

(The Chaldean method is probably not much different from astrology in its present popular form, with the possible exception that it also uses a "numerological" meaning of numbers—i.e., numerology or divination through interpretation of numbers.)

PSYCHIC: How do you use it?

DIXON: I use it for the astrology column I am writing for the newspapers. Because of the huge amount of fan mail I receive, I cannot possibly answer each letter individually. So I do the column as a guideline for the many people who write to me. I think it's good, and it's strictly scientific, but then being psychic helps a little bit, too.

PSYCHIC: Then you feel the stars have significant bearing on a person's life, beginning with the year, month, day he's born—kind of a map?

DIXON: Yes. I believe this. Take the elements that affect the ocean. Well, why shouldn't they also affect us? An example of this mood change. You get up one day and feel great, yet don't know why. That's because the elements are in your favor or there is a beneficial conjunction of the planets.

PSYCHIC: You talk about vibrations quite frequently. What do you mean?

DIXON: I really don't know, just as I don't know what electricity is. To me though, vibrations are reactions to life itself. Everybody has them; you would not be alive if you didn't.

PSYCHIC: Do you see as well as feel vibrations?

DIXON: As I mentioned earlier when we talked about tipping fingers, sometimes they're visualized, yes. It could happen unexpectedly, though, by a person's color aura coming in. But I have no control over it.

PSYCHIC: Then you also see vibrations as light, in color?

DIXON: Yes, and they could be different colors. To me they might reveal that someone perhaps is reaching for you or that something is going to happen around you. Now *what* this is I do not know; I don't know what you call it.

PSYCHIC: What about other people with talents somewhat similar to yours? Do you ever meet with them to discuss this, to learn what they feel? Is there a consensus?

DIXON: If there is a consensus, I don't know what it is. You see, I have been by myself; I've just been very busy in my life. There are probably some people with a talent far greater than mine, too, since no two people in the universe are alike.

PSYCHIC: What about the parapsychologists who are devoted to researching and understanding abilities such as yours and other psychic phenomena? Have you ever worked with any?

DIXON: The only one I have ever worked with is Dr. Riesenman, a psychiatrist here in Washington. He has called me several times on a couple of projects. One was the Jackson murder case, which I meditated on. And the Lord gave it to me.

But, you see, my life is so busy. I couldn't possibly get to all the requests I receive even if I were ten people.

Remember I have a living to make, too; I have to take care of myself, my health, and my home, just like anyone else; otherwise I would be of no good to anybody.

PSYCHIC: Have you ever been a research subject for a particular project inside or outside the laboratory?

DIXON: No, I haven't been a "guinea pig," because to me you don't turn this on and off. It's just there, stronger some days than others. And let me again stress, I don't have the time.

PSYCHIC: You're no doubt aware that many dedicated scientists have actually accumulated evidence, and recorded and evaluated it, in an effort to bring the public as well as their skeptical colleagues meaningful material in an attempt to understand psychic phenomena on a tangible level. What is your feeling about the scientific approach to investigating, evaluating, and trying to understand all this?

DIXON: I have a great respect for the scientific field and I think these scientists deserve credit, because I believe that the elements of the psychic world can be measured—to some extent. So you see, the scientists should work on this, and if I had time, I would work with them.

PSYCHIC: Do you think that these scientific data, then, are going to help support your own philosophy and eventually help to give man a better understanding of himself and the universe?

DIXON: Yes. And there's going to be a breakthrough on the cosmic ray from outer space; I have a feeling that Russia has it, the cosmic ray, which we need for ourselves and all other living things upon this earth.

So we will be very grateful to our scientists. You see, the Lord has given these men their gifts for balance upon this earth. He knows what He's doing; *we're* the ones who get everything mixed up.

PSYCHIC: Since you believe in eternal life, that is, life after death, it seems . . .

DIXON: I believe that we go back to this Holy Trinity; that your soul is your soul throughout eternity. And regarding the dead, it's through this Holy Trinity that your loved ones can ever communicate with you . . . not through séances . . . but through this one point of communication, no other way. You can't force it through séances. To me *that's* evil. I may be all wrong, but I think it's evil.

PSYCHIC: Do you think man is beginning to develop a higher awareness about himself and the universe, that he's evolving into a more intuitive and sensitive creature?

DIXON: Some, yes, and some, well, they are going in the opposite direction. They are being led away by outside influences, or I should say, other forces are having an effect on them.

I'm talking now about the campus disturbances and race riots, which I believe are organized and directed by the organization geniuses of the U.S.S.R. and also Red China. And many youngsters are joining in because they think it's the thing to do, but it's really because of these outside influences.

But in thirty-two years (the year 2,000) there is going to be a *tremendous* happening, which I talk about in detail in my new book coming out soon. And when this occurs, the Jewish people will say it's the coming of their Messiah and the Christians will say it's the second coming of Christ. I received this as a revelation.

PSYCHIC: You have a Star of David in your left hand and a star which reaches out in all directions in your right. Palm readers apparently place a great deal of significance in this for you. What is your opinion?

DIXON: Well, my opinion about palmistry is that every doctor should study and learn to read palms, because I think they are a network of one's brain.

As for my hands, they show that when the Lord breathed the breath of life into my soul He gave me the mind of an old person, not a young one. But I don't call that reincarnation.

PSYCHIC: What's the reason some of your predictions do not come true?

DIXON: Let me again refer to St. Thomas Aquinas, who said that some events—the man-willed or planned, that is, telepathy—can change from the time they are picked up to when they happen. When this happens, there's nothing I can do about it. As for misinterpreting symbols, certainly I misinterpret sometimes.

PSYCHIC: Often when predicting you do not give specific times or dates, merely stating approximate periods of time. Why?

DIXON: Timing is most difficult, unless I get the exact date and the exact time. Sometimes, for instance, I say two or three years because I have to measure it by the feel. Now sometimes I do get the exact time, as in the assassination of President Kennedy. That was a revelation; it was given to the exact day.

But in the psychic world, this is difficult. If I am given a good indication of time, though, then I am usually nearly correct.

PSYCHIC: Is there any one statement that you feel describes your philosophy or your feelings about your life and your unusual ability?

DIXON: I think I have given a pretty good idea about this from what we've already discussed. But there is one thing I'd like to pass on, if I may, a prayer on the back of my prayer card:

> I know not by what methods rare,
> But this I know—God answers prayer,
> I know not when He sends the word
> That tells us fervent prayer is heard.
> I know it cometh—soon or late;
> Therefore we need to pray and wait.
> I know not if the blessing sought
> Will come in just the way I thought.
> I leave my prayers with Him alone,
> Whose Will is wiser than my own.
>
> Anonymous

This I know, too, because I asked for something else in life. *Believe me,* what I prayed for was not what I got. Instead, God has given me something greater than I ever dreamed. I never dreamed that Presidents would call me, or that the Lord would give me revelations, or that I would be the subject of a best seller.

two
Arthur Ford

Arthur Ford was born before the turn of the century in the small seaside community of Titusville, Florida, where his boyhood centered around the Baptist Church. His father, Albert Ford, was a captain of a steamboat. He describes his mother as very Baptist.

Arthur Ford had planned to enter the ministry of the Baptist Church, but at the age of sixteen, because of "heretical notions," he was invited to leave. He subsequently joined the Disciples of Christ Church and at seventeen enrolled as a ministerial student at Transylvania University in Lexington, Kentucky. Eight years later, after an interruption for service in World War I, he was ordained a minister.

As a second lieutenant at Camp Grant, Arthur Ford's reaction to his first psychic experience was fright. He dreamed of seeing a roster of his men who died from the influenza epidemic: the roster issued that day contained the dreamed names in exact order.

His unsettling precognitive dreaming continued and extended to men killed at the front. Unnerved about these experiences he wrote his mother to find out if there were insanity in the family. An "unbalanced" aunt, he later learned, was actually a medium.

After the service, Ford returned to Transylvania University, where he found a sympathetic professor who encouraged him to develop his psychic potential. While serving for a time as a minister in a Kentucky parish, he married. The marriage, however, was short-lived.

In 1924 he went to New York to begin platform demonstrations of his developing clairvoyance. And it was there while in a meditation group with the Indian Swami Yogananda that a trance control with a French-Canadian accent announced himself as "Fletcher."

In 1927 the Rev. Mr. Ford traveled to London to meet the leading figure of Spiritualism, Sir Arthur Conan Doyle, who asked him to step onto the lecture platform to give a demonstration of clairvoyance. The next day, Conan Doyle published this statement: "One of the most amazing things I have ever seen in forty-one years of psychic experience was the demonstration of Arthur Ford." Conan Doyle urged the young sensitive to become a professional medium.

In 1928 Arthur Ford became a world-known name—practically overnight. Through Fletcher, he was credited with cracking the post-mortem Houdini code—a secret code used in Houdini's mentalist act with his wife, Beatrice. Praise, denouncement, and controversy still link the names of Ford and Houdini.

In 1931 a tragic auto crash left Ford's sister dead and him in a hospital with severe injuries. His intense pain was eased with morphine, and because his young doctor became interested in its effect on his psychic abilities, the medium left the hospital an addict. In an effort to overcome his addiction, he took the advice of another doctor who suggested the moderate use of alcohol to compensate, which, paradoxically, left him an alcoholic. He wrote in his autobi-

ography Nothing So Strange *(1958):* "It took some twenty years and a lot of suffering and humiliation before I overcame . . . the need of alcohol."

Nevertheless, during those years Arthur Ford managed to produce high-quality work with many prominent psychical researchers, including Professor William McDougall at Duke University, the writer Upton Sinclair, and more recently, W. G. Roll of the Psychical Research Foundation.

Traveling to many countries, Ford found wide acceptance of his mediumship, especially among the English clergymen who formed the Churches' Fellowship for Psychical Studies. In 1955 he became instrumental in forming a similar group of clergymen in this country, the Spiritual Frontiers Fellowship.

A long-time resident of Philadelphia, Arthur Ford made his final home in Miami, Florida, where he died in January, 1971.

PSYCHIC: You have been called "The World's Greatest Medium." Do you think you are?
FORD: No, I'm not. Any medium, if he is the right one for the sitter, can be the greatest medium in the world for that person. I don't feel flattered by that at all. In fact, it rather embarrasses me. But one thing I have learned is: Never believe your own press notices.
PSYCHIC: When did your trance mediumship begin?
FORD: Toward the end of 1924, when I was in a meditation group in New York with Swami Yogananda. I went into a trance, or "complete detachment," as Yogananda called it. Suddenly I began to talk with a French accent. The voice said his name was Fletcher and told who he was.
PSYCHIC: Who do you think Fletcher is?
FORD: He was a French-Canadian Catholic boy that I had played with when I was about five years old in Florida. His family was spending the winter there. My mother objected to me playing with him because they were Catholic. We were Baptists, you see. But I

was fascinated with them because they were always talking about the saints.

After Fletcher had come through several times and told where his family lived, I went to look them up. He had been killed in the First World War and his brother gave me a picture of him. We use his middle name of "Fletcher," since his family, which includes several priests, wouldn't want their name used.

PSYCHIC: Did Fletcher ever explain why he came?

FORD: He said he was working out his own problems. He was always raising the devil about things I shouldn't do. I used to drink and smoke too much. I had to give them both up. On several occasions Fletcher said, "I have to stick with Ford as long as he needs me, but I wish he would die so I can get loose."

PSYCHIC: Do you think we all have such guardians?

FORD: I think we do. Maybe we don't know it, but I think that some loved ones are interested in us. They're not "supernatural beings"— if it happens, it must be natural—they're just people who have loved you or are interested in you, or else are drawn to you because you are doing something that they were doing.

PSYCHIC: What sort of work do you do as a medium?

FORD: A great deal of our work is done with psychiatrists. Some psychiatrists are coming around to believe that invading personalities can cause a lot of trouble. Then, too, if the patient can't remember what started a trauma, the psychiatrist can't help him. Yet he may have a deceased grandmother or father or mother who knows what happened. And then Fletcher brings the person who belongs to the patient to tell what happened. And the doctor is there as well.

PSYCHIC: How does your psychic work differ from working in trance with Fletcher to working consciously?

FORD: When Fletcher comes through, my conscious mind is completely out. So I don't consciously color the information. But everything that comes through me must be colored to some extent by what I know or what I think. I don't get words, just symbols and ideas that have to be interpreted.

I don't do conscious clairvoyance anymore because it suddenly

dawned on me that I was being dishonest. At public demonstrations with a crowd of a thousand people, anything you say will fit *someone* in the crowd. So I quit that about twenty years ago. That's the reason I'm not very popular with the Spiritualists. When a Spiritualist puts a dollar in the collection, he wants a dollar's worth of spooks.
PSYCHIC: Then you are not a Spiritualist?
FORD: Yes, I am, but in the real sense of spiritualism as a philosophy. But not as a cultist or sectarian. But I do give the Spiritualists credit for keeping the subject alive until the scientists were compelled to look at it.

The worst thing that ever happened to the Spiritualist movement was when they organized into a church. If you have a church, you can do anything—and the law can't touch you. It became a religious cloak for the charlatan. But now, the Spiritualist Church in this country is practically dead.
PSYCHIC: Why do you think it died?
FORD: Well, for one thing, so many of the "spirits" are so ridiculous. What a picture it makes: a great big fat woman or fat man—like me—with a little girl control talking baby talk. That doesn't go down. Also the growth of neo-Pentecostalism growing up in the old-line churches is largely responsible for the decline of the Spiritualist churches.
PSYCHIC: You have had only Fletcher and no other control?
FORD: Yes.
PSYCHIC: What kind of survival evidence has Fletcher brought through you?
FORD: In every sitting with Fletcher, he gets things that the sitter doesn't know, but has to check out. That rules out telepathy or mind-reading from the sitter. In the early days of my mediumship, most of my sitters were critical investigators, and Fletcher got into the habit of doing this for them. Suppose a grandmother comes and is trying to prove to you who she is. If she gives the name of somebody she knew but that you didn't know, then you have to check it out, and that eliminates the idea of mind-reading.

For instance, a woman sitter came with a thimble that had belonged to her late grandmother. Now Fletcher gave this woman a message that didn't make any sense to her at all. He said the thimble belonged to a certain woman whom he described and gave an initial of her name. Well, the sitter played the tape of the sitting for her mother, who said, "That's right. That thimble was given to your grandmother by the woman Fletcher described."

One sitter who always checked everything out was Bishop James Pike. Some of the things that were the most convincing were so intimate and personal that he didn't print them in his book *The Other Side*.

PSYCHIC: What do you think convinced Bishop Pike that his dead son communicated through you?

FORD: I think the thing that convinced Bishop Pike that he was getting messages from his son was not the séance we televised in Toronto. That wasn't done live, you see. I wouldn't go on the air live, because you can't turn it on that way. I agreed to it only if it were done quietly with just the bishop and Allen Spraggett, religion editor of the *Toronto Star*, who arranged it. Then Bishop Pike checked out what I said, and cut out some of the more intimate things about his life. It was two weeks before the program was shown.

About two months later, Bishop Pike and his wife-to-be, Diane, came for a sitting at my home in Philadelphia. It was during that sitting that Bishop Pike's son told about the people whom the bishop was able to check out. Diane told me that he probably would not have written *The Other Side* if it hadn't been for that second sitting.

PSYCHIC: What psychic impressions did you have when Bishop Pike was missing in the Judean desert in 1969?

FORD: The only message I got about Pike was on Tuesday. You remember that Diane had left him to go for help the day before, the first of September. I was in New York recovering from a heart attack. My nurse was with me. I heard over the radio that Pike was missing, and I went into deep meditation to see if I could get anything. I got that he was alive in a cave at that time. He needed help of course.

I called a friend in the news division of ABC, who relayed the message to Diane Pike in Jerusalem, and she got the message on

Tuesday night. The newspapers, however, kept reprinting this, saying that I said he was alive on Saturday. Diane telephoned her younger brother Jim in California, and asked him to see if I could get any further information. But I couldn't get anything more. Diane says in her book *Search* that it was entirely possible that Pike was alive and in a cave or some shady place when I had that impression on Tuesday.

On Sunday morning the troops went out looking for him again. Diane wasn't going; she had given up. She felt that she would know if he were dead, but they couldn't find him. That night she had a vision in which she saw him leaving the body, ascending to a great crowd of people. She drew a sketch of the scene and shortly afterward they found him. A photograph taken of the place where they found his body matched her vision almost exactly.

PSYCHIC: Why do you think she didn't have the vision earlier while he was still alive?

FORD: I think probably because he was so confused and mentally gone, suffering from dehydration. It was an extraordinary thing, but he couldn't reach her until he was mentally clear. And that must have happened when he fell to his death in a canyon.

PSYCHIC: Has Bishop Pike come through you since his death?

FORD: No. I haven't given but four sittings in the last year. I have been very ill. The doctor doesn't want me to do sittings, because when I go into trance I induce the very condition he is treating me for.

One sitting was for an astronaut who came anonymously. I didn't know who he was at the time of the sitting. Afterward, he wrote me a very beautiful letter in which he said everything checked out. Another sitting was for a senator who is an active member of Spiritual Frontiers. The others were for doctors.

PSYCHIC: Do you know if any other mediums made contact with Bishop Pike?

FORD: Diane Pike told me she had a few sittings with mediums, including a very good one with Ena Twigg in England. But she is getting letters from all sorts of mediums who want to get into the act. A great many of these letters started before the bishop passed on.

One said, for instance, "I am the only medium your son says he can contact you through." But the bishop didn't take that very seriously, since his son had communicated through Mrs. Twigg, George Daisley, and myself.

PSYCHIC: Have you ever had experience with any fraudulent mediums?

FORD: Yes. I have come across frauds. When people started telling them they're wonderful, they believed it. They got greedy, egotistical, and unbearable. Then they tried to force it—but you can't turn it on like that. I made a rule all my life that if I couldn't get anything, just to say so, and try again. And people seem to respect me for that. But if some poor woman has a husband and kids to support, and she sees five or ten bucks coming through the door, she's going to try to get it. And so she gets a bad reputation.

I don't think anyone ever starts out as a fraud. There isn't enough money in it to make a person deliberately choose it. For instance, I don't make my living by mediumship. I have inherited Florida real estate from my father.

PSYCHIC: How did the publicity from the Bishop Pike séance affect your career?

FORD: It cost me a lot of money. The first month after the televised séance, I received over twelve thousand letters. I had to hire extra typists to answer them. I still get about two hundred letters a week. Often people are in trouble, or they want advice on where to find a medium. I feel I must answer anyone who takes the trouble to write me.

PSYCHIC: What emphasis do you think psychical research should pursue?

FORD: The older group of psychical researchers were trying to prove survival through physical phenomena. And, of course, that was a materialistic thing, and it didn't work. And most of the fraudulent mediums were the ones who went out for physical phenomena, and that is true today. Then, when Professor William McDougall came to Duke University from Harvard, things took a different turn. McDougall became interested in a study of consciousness. I had many sittings for Professor McDougall. McDougall was the man who trained J. B. Rhine, you know.

Now Rhine has done a great job, but he stopped short of the survival question. Rhine set up his own standards, and if you didn't meet that standard, you were out. Now other parapsychologists, like Ian Stevenson and W. G. Roll, let things happen and then study them. They don't try to make them happen in a certain way. Rhine has coined a phrase that I like very much and I think that's the direction psychical research is going in: the study of the total nature of man; not just the study of psychical phenomena.

PSYCHIC: It would seem you feel that psychic phenomena fit in with the rest of man's experience.

FORD: Yes. I think it is a universal thing.

PSYCHIC: Then how do you think spirituality is related to the psychic?

FORD: Some of the best psychics I have known have also been some of the worst reprobates I have known. Some of the most religious people you ever met are not spiritual in any sense. Some of the most spiritual people have never had any interest whatever in religion.

Religion is all man-made; spirituality is something within you. Spiritual values are something you learn. And the conflict in us between "God" and the "Devil" is actually a conflict between our animal heritage, which is instinct, and our acquired spiritual values. Sometimes, instinct gets on top.

Personally, I don't think a man should be condemned in the slightest if he once in a while slips down to the animal level, because all men do. Now the word "psychic" pertains to the soul or the breath of God, so you could say it is something we are born with.

PSYCHIC: Would you encourage people to develop their psychic gifts?

FORD: Yes. The day of the professional medium is about over. We've been useful as guinea pigs. Through us, scientists have learned something about the conditions necessary for it to happen.

I have taught a great many groups and find they all have some spiritual gift. Any group of seven to eight people who take time to listen and read, to understand the techniques involved, and practice faithfully will generally have some psychic experience within a few months. One or two of them may become very good psychics. Spiritual Frontiers has groups like this all over the country. And you would be surprised at how many clergymen are developing their psychic gifts.

PSYCHIC: Have any psychics come out of these groups?

FORD: Oh yes, a lot of them. I don't think they are going to be professionals. As I said, the day of the professional psychic is over. But these people get together and they meditate and they share, and they have a concern for each other. And they are faithful and devout about it as dedicated human beings.

PSYCHIC: Do you think everyone develops in the same way?

FORD: No. Everyone has his own individual "mental set," his specialty for psychic insight, whether it be art, writing, spiritual healing, spiritual service, science, prophecy, or communication with the spirits of the departed. And who is to say which gift is greatest? Paul said it was the gift of love. Jesus implied it was doing the will of the Father.

PSYCHIC: What about any dangers in developing psychically?

FORD: People who go into this without spiritual aspirations should be warned that unless they remain open-minded about the possibility of being led into deeper meanings of life, their experience will almost certainly turn out to be a blind alley.

For people who covet psychic potency out of profit and power, my advice is unequivocal: either develop higher motivation or drop the whole business at once. The consequences of deliberate misuse of these abilities can be disastrous.

PSYCHIC: As an ordained minister, do you foresee any progress regarding the spiritual realm?

FORD: Yes. I think we are getting back more like the early church, where small groups got together. The underground churches were in a real sense spiritual frontiers as long ago as that. And now these small groups are rediscovering these early principles. But I think the day of the professional preacher is almost over, too. The whole institution of organized religion has followed the pattern of the secular government. But it has come to an impasse.

Remember, too, that most of our theological systems developed in a prescientific age. But now science has destroyed the concept that earth is all there is. I think the two great projects of the immediate future will be the exploration of outer space and the exploration of inner man.

PSYCHIC: Has there ever been any conflict in your life between Arthur Ford, the preacher, and Arthur Ford, the medium?

FORD: I don't know. When I was first studying to become a preacher, I didn't know anything about psychical phenomena. If they talked about it in those days, it was only to do with the devil. And before I was in Disciples of Christ Church, I was a Baptist. I'll bet you didn't know I was kicked out of the Baptist Church for heresy at the age of sixteen. Best thing that ever happened to me.

But I love the church, and I haven't left it. I just grew out of a belief in the old theology into a larger realm. I'm still a preacher, and I'm still preaching. I preach to preachers.

PSYCHIC: What do you preach to them?

FORD: To get off that bag of dogma, take a look at what's going on in the universe, and not be ashamed of their heritage of psychical phenomena.

Too many ministers these days have an "Edifice Complex." All they want to do is build churches. Half the churches in America are new churches, but they're yet to be paid for. Their membership is declining. They're forgetting about the real purpose of religion, and they're becoming active in lots of things the state can do in a better way. Those are important things, but that isn't the prime duty of the church.

PSYCHIC: What do you think it is?

FORD: To give people a sense of meaning, a sense of something more than just *this*. The church will die unless it has a rebirth of spirituality. That's what really counts—not the dances or basketball games or rock groups. Young people are hungering for spiritual sustenance, and if the church is to survive, it must give it to them.

The only church that is really growing is the Pentecostal Church. They are a noisy bunch, but they believe in the Holy Spirit and they believe in healing, and they believe in being happy about it. And they talk in tongues. But that is one of the gifts of the spirit mentioned by St. Paul.

PSYCHIC: Why do you think so many churches think psychic gifts are of the devil?

FORD: A lot of churches have attacked me, saying that I was corrupting the church, that I was an Antichrist, a devil in disguise, and all that. Some reporter once asked me if I wanted to answer that charge. I said I never engaged in arguments like that. And he said, "Well, if you did, what would you say?" And like a fool, I told him and he printed it. I didn't mean for him to. I said, "Well, if what I say comes from the devil, at least the people know what the hell I'm talking about."

PSYCHIC: What implications do you think parapsychology has for religion?

FORD: A great deal. The phenomena of religion are universal. They didn't start with Christianity. Other religions talk about spirits—both good and bad—back as far as you can go. And immortality may take many forms. But Christianity made one contribution that is unique. Christianity doesn't talk about immortality—it talks about survival. It's the only religion in the world that holds you survive, not as a part or something different, but as a total personality with memory and character, and potential for growth.

Jesus demonstrated that when He returned from the dead after three days and said, according to Peter, He had been preaching to the souls in Sheol, the Jewish afterworld. Why would He preach to them if He didn't think it would do some good?

PSYCHIC: Perhaps psychic phenomena have importance for us in this life then.

FORD: Definitely. In First Corinthians, Paul names all the spiritual gifts, and we haven't found a new one since. Paul said, "You all have this gift." And it all comes through the one Spirit manifesting through each of you individually.

His thirteenth chapter on love is more than love—it is a perfect outline of psychiatry. He says you've got to remove all negative qualities of hatred, jealousy, greed, resentment, and replace them with positive qualities of love, kindness, patience, and charity.

Then Paul tells us about the physical body and the spiritual body. They are not the same. One goes into the ground, and that's the end of it. The other one survives. But I always urge people to get straightened out here. Because why try to plunge into a new dimension of consciousness when you don't know what to do with yourself on a rainy Sunday afternoon?

PSYCHIC: How would you express your belief in God?

FORD: When people ask me if I believe in God, I say, "Certainly I believe in God—but I don't know what God is." I don't believe in the God that some of these churches talk about—a sort of Santa Claus. I think God is a creative force individualized through each and all of us. I think Jesus made it very clear when He said, "It is the Father in me who does the work."

I'm always amused by people who are searching for God, trying to find God. *God isn't lost.* They are looking in the wrong places. They should look inside themselves.

And I don't believe in a personal God who is a limited personality. But I believe in a personal God because I have had personal experiences with Him. My life has been saved three times—miraculously.

PSYCHIC: Do you feel that young people today are in any way different from older generations?

FORD: Yes. It's inevitable. In my day we didn't have things like television, movies, automobiles, and rapid means of communication. Today a twelve-year-old boy knows more things than I knew when I was thirty.

PSYCHIC: Perhaps they have more psychic awareness, too.

FORD: Yes, I think so. They are more sensitive, have more awareness. And I think it's healthy too. I have given many talks to students in high schools and colleges. Those kids quote books back to me. They know the works of J. B. Rhine and Gardner Murphy and other modern parapsychologists. And they are interested in what is going on in this field. They are disenchanted with the establishment and with organized religion. But classes in the psychology and history of religion are popular.

PSYCHIC: Some people say a new age is beginning. What is your opinion?

FORD: At the birth of Christ, the wise men saw a constellation in the sky that meant a new age, and the constellation was in Pisces. About twenty-five years ago, Pisces began to move away and Aquarius began to move in. The time of Pisces was of war and struggles. But the age of Aquarius is slowly coming up from the depths into the light. But I really don't know much about astrology.

PSYCHIC: What validity do you think astrology has?

FORD: I have never known a good astrologer who didn't say, "In order to interpret the chart, I have to be psychic." I think it is the same thing when people read cards. It's like psychometry, when I hold an object as a focus to get things about people.

PSYCHIC: What is your view of reincarnation?

FORD: I think Dr. Ian Stevenson's book *Twenty Cases Suggestive of Reincarnation* is really the only scientific study of it. It's an interesting part of the whole psychic picture; I think some people oversimplify it.

And in India, the upper classes use it as a club to hold down the lower classes. They tell them, "You were born to be poor and miserable. It is fate." That's not true. We do have free will. I don't think that there is some God keeping books on us, who might say, "Well, when Ford was Mr. Jones a hundred years ago, he did wrong, and therefore we'll break Ford's leg today."

PSYCHIC: You mean the concept of karma?

FORD: Yes. The writer Gerald Heard makes an interesting suggestion: that the theologians of the early Roman church who wanted to establish a priesthood had to deal with the idea of karma, expressed in the Jewish doctrine of "An eye for an eye, a tooth for a tooth." So these early churchmen changed the doctrine of karma into the doctrine of original sin. Jesus never said anything that suggested He knew anything about original sin. Jesus said, "You are free from the law." In other words, you live under grace, and you have free will.

Nowadays, most people who talk about karma seem to think

karma is all bad. They think their problems were caused by something wrong done in a previous life. But by accepting the principles of Christ and living by them, you can create good karma too.

PSYCHIC: Do you think God has a plan for us or do we make our own?

FORD: I think we make our own. But there is definitely a plan in the scheme of evolution, isn't there? We fit into that. But I don't think God sends us anywhere after death. We go where we choose to go. So you can't pass the buck to the Almighty.

I think that if men knew they would live beyond death, perhaps they would try to face their mistakes now and somehow overcome them.

And Swami Yogananda once said something to me that sums it up: "Fate, karma, destiny—call it what you will—there is a law of justice that determines our basic pattern, but not by chance. The important thing to realize is that while we may not escape our own basic pattern, we can work in harmony with it. That is where free will comes in. Once having chosen, a man has to accept the consequences of his choice, and go on from there."

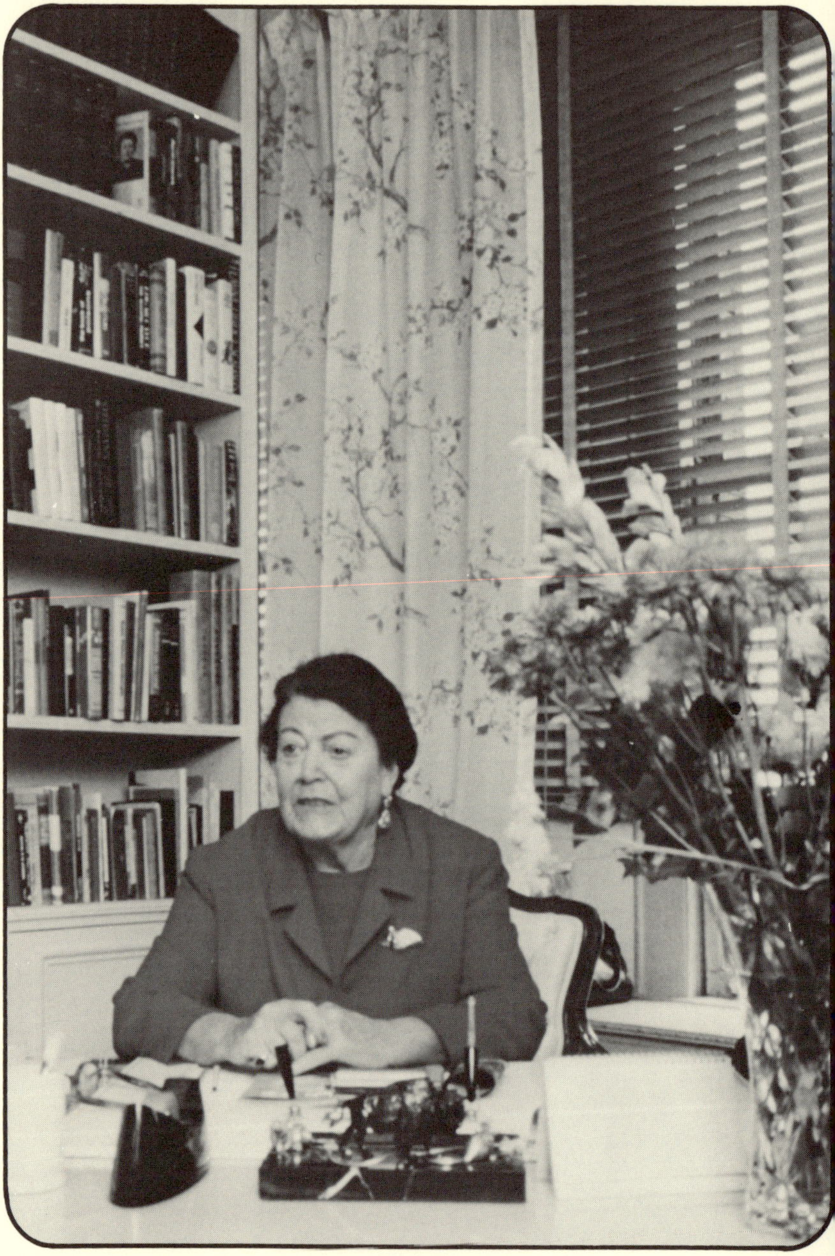

three
Eileen J. Garrett

Eileen Jeanette Garrett was born just before the turn of the century in Beau Park, County Meath, Ireland. She was raised by her uncle and aunt on their small farm in County Meath.

Much to the confusion of her foster parents and others, young Eileen's psychic side began manifesting itself at a very early age, getting her into about as much trouble as it helped her avoid during those formative years.

At the age of fifteen, following the death of her uncle and because of a delicate bronchial condition, she was sent to boarding school in the south of England. En route, however, she stopped to visit relatives in London where she met and married her first husband. To her delight the marriage also ruled out her attending boarding school.

Six years later, World War I erupted and her husband entered the service, while she remained in London. There, with a friend, she opened a small café, but later started her own hostel to care for wounded soldiers returning from the front.

Evidence of her unusual psychic gift continued to manifest itself. Precognition of the death of her two sons, a clairvoyant vision of the death of her second husband, and many incidences of a psychic nature led Mrs. Garrett to meeting with people seriously involved in the psychic field. She began studying and developing her psychic abilities at the British College of Psychic Science, under the direction of Hewat McKenzie, the founder of the college. As a result of this training, her trance mediumship fully emerged.

Mrs. Garrett continued with her psychic work in London until 1931, when an invitation was extended to her by members of the American Society for Psychical Research to visit America. Throughout the thirties, Mrs. Garrett pursued her search for an answer to her mediumship and other psychic questions, participating in research and experiments in universities in both America and Europe.

In France at the outbreak of war in 1939, Mrs. Garrett remained to work with civilians until she was forced to leave at the end of 1940. It was during the long passage from France to America that she decided to found and publish a literary magazine, and in 1941 the first issue of Tomorrow *appeared. She also established Creative Age Press to publish books, one of the first which was* Telepathy, *which she herself wrote.*

Despite a full schedule of publishing, Mrs. Garrett continued her experiments in psychical research. Not surprisingly, this subsequently led to her establishing the Parapsychology Foundation in 1951, ". . . to encourage organized research in psychic phenomena." The Foundation still supports impartial scientific inquiry, sponsors international conferences on the subject, publishes a bimonthly periodical, and makes available its extensive library to anyone wishing information on the subject.

For many years the Foundation's president and director, Mrs. Garrett said: "I have a gift, a capacity—a delusion, if you will—

called 'psychic'. . . . I have been called many things from a charlatan to a miracle woman. I am, at least, neither of these."

As a world-renowned medium and an investigator of the paranormal, in the course of her career Eileen Garrett met and worked with many well-known people deeply interested in the field—such as Sir Oliver Lodge, Sir Arthur Conan Doyle, Hereward Carrington, Carl Jung, Harry Price, Aldous Huxley. In addition, she has written many books on this as well as other subjects.

Her contributions, writing, experiments, research, and works in the field of parapsychology brought her wide acclaim and an enduring popularity. She died at Le Piol, France, in September, 1970.

PSYCHIC: What was your first memory of your psychic abilities?
GARRETT: This goes back into my very earliest childhood, but without knowing what they were. And I suppose I was a bit of a nuisance to everybody around me, because of my unusual sense—I could tell when they were telling the truth, even my teachers. I've always been observant, listening with both ears and wondering why people avoided the truth. I sensed it.

It also often kept me out of trouble with my aunt, who was a very difficult person to live with, from my point of view, although she was a great lady. She must have suffered greatly, because I was an impossible child. As I look back now, I smile over the things I did, but then I was living in a world nobody else understood.

PSYCHIC: What, psychically, was the most impressive experience for you during that period?
GARRETT: I think the loss of my uncle, who was extremely kind and understanding to me. A few weeks after his death, I was sitting in my room in the evening, feeling a bit restless and unhappy, when I saw him clearly standing before me. I was surprised at his appearance of health, since before his death he had seemed feeble and worn. But he appeared young, erect, and strong. I was overjoyed at seeing him, and he showed he was happy to see me. He asked me to obey my

aunt's wishes whenever possible, but told me he understood the difficulties of my present life with her. He then predicted that I would be free and would go to London to study in two years, which did happen. Then, he was gone before I could ask any questions.

So, when he died, something very precious went out of my life and then I came into direct contact with death. It's probably when I began looking at death from every point of view.

PSYCHIC: What kind of impact did this have, realizing you could see things others couldn't.

GARRETT: It had a terrible impact on me. Yet I knew when I saw something, I really had seen it. So it was no good telling me that I was making up stories. This, I suppose, is what hardened me and gave me a sense of myself.

My uncle was a great help, too. He was a very tolerant man, with a lot of wit and humor, and I looked to him for everything. When I told him strange things that I had seen, he listened and would say, "Well, my child, maybe so, who knows." He never said this was wrong or right, so I would take him all kinds of stories about people who had died. He had lived in India a great deal of his life, and in his own way, was extremely sensitive. He never in any sense tried to make it seem that I was telling an untruth.

So, you see, I had come to conclusions about myself and this was very important for me. I don't think many children have to face up to that kind of thing. Yet at a very early age I knew things and would tell them to the people concerned, becoming a bit of a nuisance in the process, and they would say, "God help us. There, she's off again."

PSYCHIC: I suppose this was confusing to you as well as others.

GARRETT: Certainly, but you couldn't understand that kind of a child. Yet in a way it gave me a kind of power. I didn't know what it was. I only knew that people seemed to avoid conversation in my presence.

It got me into trouble in other ways, too. Once my aunt punished me for what she thought was a prank I had played on her. I had seen her sister, my Aunt Leone, who lived twenty miles away, coming up the walk unannounced and carrying a baby. As I recall, Aunt Leone said to me, "I am going away now, and must take the baby with me." I ran to tell my aunt and when we got to the door, Aunt Leone was not to be found, even though I made a thorough search. My aunt punished me for concocting such a story. But several days later news came of Aunt Leone's death, while giving birth to a child who also died.

To get even with my aunt, I went down to the pond and deliberately, one by one, drowned her little ducklings, which were her pride. But a strange thing occurred, while watching the little dead bodies, a gray, smokelike substance rose up from each one. It was like a nebulous, fluid stuff that rose and curled, moving out and away from the lifeless forms. My fear gave way to astonishment, and I became joyful, because I thought the ducklings were coming back to life. But, of course, they didn't.

PSYCHIC: Was anyone in your family psychic besides yourself?

GARRETT: Yes, I had an aunt who had a great reputation as a healer, although I have no idea how psychic she was. People within a radius of fifty miles who had heard of her—that was a good distance in Ireland then—would send for her because of this healing power.

PSYCHIC: The facets of your psychic ability—healing, clairvoyance, seeing auras, and so on—were these manifested at the outset?

GARRETT: Yes, and somehow I was aware of them. For instance, I knew it because of the way in which I got to know what people were saying—how much you could believe and how it really happened. It was a knowing—an inner conviction.

PSYCHIC: Do you think that your psychic abilities are interconnected in some fashion, that there is a central seat to them?

GARRETT: There must be. There must be an acute sensory feeling. I think, too, there's a lot of animal in my makeup. For example, I would go out at night and smell the atmosphere to know what it would be like the next day. I could smell bad weather. I could also smell if someone had been in my room, which I can do to this day.

Animals have this unusual faculty. They can smell something threatening and are so much more aware in these areas than most of us.

PSYCHIC: Perhaps every human being possesses this psychic seat to the extent that it is an integral part of all of us, waiting to be developed?

GARRETT: I think so. I think that conventions with which we are raised have suppressed it, too. If I were to have listened to all the conventional things as I was supposed to, I would have become an awful hypocrite. And I think that happens to many people. Thank heavens I never had this, though.

Yet, I'm more discreet in what I say now, although as a child I would spontaneously reveal what I sensed, saying, "Oh, that's not the way it happened," and it often didn't sit well with my elders, particularly in Ireland, where more than anywhere they like to embellish when telling a story.

So I became very familiar with my sensitivity, but I do not think it is so unusual. We all have it—only of course we grow up and go to our parents first, who usually say, "Don't bother me; don't talk like that, you're telling stories." So you become a little fearful, afraid, and possibly ashamed, and you don't do anything about it.

Businessmen have often told me they have achieved their successes because they negated this type of intimidation, following instead their strong inner feelings.

PSYCHIC: What would you say to a parent who has a child with an ability such as yours?

GARRETT: I would advise parents to make friends with the child at an early age and to get down, in a sense, to where the child lives. If the child tells you this and that, as children will, be positive not negative, and discuss it with him then or at an appropriate time.

I also think the parent must have love and understanding enough to deal with a child and this is what is lacking today. The parents think it's enough to give money and let the children have a good time. Children don't want that. It's the love, understanding, and the affection—and by affection I mean that the child trusts you.

In other words, you get to the point where you are friends and where they know they can talk to you of anything. That is important and healthy, for both the parents and the children.

PSYCHIC: You underwent special psychic training in your early life, what specifically?

GARRETT: I spent five years training with Hewat McKenzie at the British College of Psychic Science in London. We became excellent friends. He was an eminent psychical researcher of his day, a man of great self-assurance and yet with a great sensitivity. He helped me develop my trance state, kept the experiments and sittings objective, and discovered the controls—"Uvani" and "Abdul Latif."

But with regard to training, I think if you train for anything—whether to become a doctor, teacher, lawyer—you have to give your time to it. In all, I gave ten years of rigid training to all aspects of this, which is quite a lot of time.

Sometimes we would have sittings in which I never saw the person for whom it was arranged, sometimes we went out to disturbed houses, where there were poltergeists. Then there was the lengthy training in trance sessions, working with hypnosis, and preparing myself for the ability to go into deep trance.

PSYCHIC: Was this special training the reason you have generally pursued a scientific instead of a religious approach to psychic phenomena?

GARRETT: Oh, it had no religious effect at all. When Mr. McKenzie told me I was able to become a medium, I looked at him with suspicion. It was unlikely that anybody could influence me to be anything I did not wish to be. But thank heaven, I was able to look at myself and think that I would go along with him, because he made sense.

Yet, it was difficult at times. He would keep me working until three or four in the morning, and I would come out of trance and tell him in no uncertain terms that I didn't think I was supposed to work until *that* hour of the morning.

Having worked with him, I think I took a great deal more from his point of view than from the point of view of anybody else. I came to the conclusion that what we were doing was something that mattered intensely and that when I went off deep into the subconscious mind and produced the alleged entities, this was part of my life. So I accepted it and endeavored to keep it at a high level.

McKenzie started the British College of Psychic Science, you know. He wouldn't permit his workers to meet, even though there were many people in the college, and he was training and working with six mediums at the time, among them Mrs. Gladys Osborne Leonard. When he died, his wife carried on, and since I had a very healthy respect for her, I continued to work at the college until I came to America. I worked for some time with the American Society for Psychical Research here.

PSYCHIC: What do you think is the reason for the widespread and growing interest in psychic phenomena today?

GARRETT: I wish I could give you an answer to that. In a sense, though, it's amazing, because at any time in my early life when you mentioned anything about psychic work, the police might call on you.

At that time, of course, it was a very difficult thing to say anything about being psychic. Yet we went on, and McKenzie put it on the map as something with a relationship to science that should be studied.

I think he knew that one day this would have to be taken into account, and that there would be an acceptance of things psychic. And I always remember his serious attitude toward it, that this was a gift, a sacred gift, and it must only be used to help people who need help. And so I followed his direction, and I have continued to do so.

But I think that the current popularity is natural and that it was bound to happen. People were frightened of it, for one thing, and they were a bit frightened of anyone who knew much about it, let alone displayed it.

Yet on the other hand, they got it all mixed up with their tea leaves and their fortune-telling.

PSYCHIC: Yes, but tea leaves, crystal balls, cards, and the like have long been associated with some genuine aspects of the field, such as clairvoyance and precognition; how do you account for that?

GARRETT: These methods probably serve as a form of concentration which allows the unconscious to reveal inner aspects of the mind. They are perhaps as old as man himself and must be respected.

PSYCHIC: What is your opinion of astrology and the so-called Age of Aquarius?

GARRETT: I really haven't given it very much thought, and I admit to very little knowledge about astrological terminology. I don't think I can offer any opinion here. I keep it out of my life; I have felt no need or desire to include it.

PSYCHIC: Then what about numerology, palmistry, and other such occult practices, where do they fit in your study of the psychic field?

GARRETT: Well, I have not shut them out, but I have not pursued them with any avid interest, either. As a matter of fact, I can read palms. I used to do it for youngsters to amuse them, though not as a serious pursuit. But I do think there are lines, certain pictures in the hands of everyone, that display something of an individual's temperament.

PSYCHIC: You have mentioned numerology in your writings on several occasions, selecting addresses because the numbers were "right." What about this?

GARRETT: I practice numerology as a kind of guideline when I wish to be certain of some particular aspect that touches my own life. Numbers will present themselves to me spontaneously, and since they come of their own accord, I use them in an oblique way for my own guidance.

PSYCHIC: Then how does numerology blend into your concept of the scheme of things, its significance to the psychic world?

GARRETT: I think it is a fascinating study but one which I have not had time to follow seriously myself. I do feel certain that numbers have a profound meaning of their own in the life of any person. Very often when I am talking with somebody who needs help, the numbers of days, or months, or years may flash across my mind, and so I have to use them spontaneously. I'm sure numerology has its own scientific basis in the occult.

PSYCHIC: You have definite views that "physiological centers are vitally important to the psychic." What do you mean by this?

GARRETT: I believe that areas such as the solar plexis are where I first sense things, not within the "thinking part" of my brain. I must get away from objective thinking and allow the subjective areas of the mind to reveal the answer. When this happens, you don't monitor what you're saying, because you're living with an inner voice. You are looking deep within the self, which I have come to regard as the seat of inspiration. It's all in the region of the solar plexis.

PSYCHIC: Does this include the spot between your eyebrow, popularly called the third eye, where you have said images register?

GARRETT: Yes, yes. People talk of the third eye, but I think that it is in the back of the head, the ancient brain. When you begin to get things happening in the solar plexis, they'll register in the old brain and then come through in the third-eye area, as mental pictures. And I feel that these areas of the body reveal certain levels of inner experience, which can be translated to the benefit of those who seek answers or help.

PSYCHIC: Do you think that psychedelic drugs help manifest psychic abilities in any way?

GARRETT: No. And I don't feel the necessity of taking drugs of any type to see what they would do to aid the psychic aspect, although I have taken them, but only under test conditions. There is a whole series of writings on these experiments.

I think drugs are very detrimental to most people, because they can be so frightening. The great trouble with LSD is that it opens the door to reveal certain aspects of the self not otherwise understood. Not many of us can face our real selves, you know. This is what causes the trouble.

PSYCHIC: You have said that with your experiences, "it would be impossible to doubt the continuity of consciousness and the survival of the human entity after death." Do you still feel this way?

GARRETT: Oh, I think an immortal spirit is there. But call it what you will. It's there in the process of evolution.

The whole process of evolution begins way, way back and goes on. We have to go through all these experiences, I think, and heaven knows for how long, until we reach a perfect consciousness. Maybe

that is an end in itself. But there is no ending to the life forces. I believe there is more than just a vital spark that burns out.
PSYCHIC: What about the individual consciousness?
GARRETT: Well, I think that the individual consciousness eventually becomes absorbed into the great nirvana. We haven't lived in vain; we haven't lived for ourselves. We have lived because we are a part of a great scheme and we each have something to contribute to that universal cosmos.
PSYCHIC: Is your conclusion about the continuum of conscious man a result of your ability to see discarnate beings?
GARRETT: I have seen so many people who have come back, talked with so many people, sat with so many people, that I would say so. I have been working as a sensitive, as a medium, for fifty years. And it is my conclusion that the information obtained through my psychic abilities, so many facts concerning so many people, must be contained in the cosmos.
PSYCHIC: Then you must have a philosophy about the purpose of life.
GARRETT: To me the whole of life is an experiment to be lived out as best we can. Life should be met with responsibility. If it's going to be joyful or sad, or whatever it is, we have to live it. It is part of the way in which we must develop, and we shouldn't sidestep it.

So, you see, we have definite contributions to make and we must absolutely make them at the best level we can. This I believe.
PSYCHIC: Then you think that life is part of a great plan?
GARRETT: Yes. Whatever we undertake is for development and it must be undertaken with responsibility. And what we always have to have is self-respect. Never mind what anybody thinks, we must know ourselves and respect what we know. This is growth and we must be here for some purpose—I believe it's greater than we can ever think of.

You know, we don't just grow up and have misfortunes and difficulties, get the old stuff laid aside, then put a few flowers on the grave and forget about it. That's not life at all. There must be a greater order than we can conceive of—to the whole aspect of being. We have to go, I think, through all kinds of experiences and perhaps after we go, we have to meet another set of circumstances for which we have been prepared or ill-prepared here.

But whether we have liked it or not, we have to go through with it, because the experiment of being is all important to a Godhead we don't even comprehend.

PSYCHIC: Is this the "Universal Mind" you often refer to in your writings, your concept of a Supreme Being?

GARRETT: As a relation to the Supreme Being on our way to our own form, if you like to call it supremacy. We're never finished learning.

I think there comes a time when the individual or the "it" has to be thrown out into the world and if "it" doesn't survive, "it" must try again and again.

Each one, you see, has his place and should be fulfilling it as well as he knows how, working out something. And in the process he makes difficulties for himself that he will have to define and deal with at some time—whether now or later. And the worse we are, the more building we have to do.

PSYCHIC: This sounds like the philosophy of reincarnation.

GARRETT: In a sense—the broadest sense—I don't believe in reincarnation the way in which some people do—that I was Madame So-and-So or some great personage. But certainly what knowledge that I have has come not by the virtue of this one life, but of many experiences.

Also, I have the belief that nothing happens by happenstance. Things are ordered and we do them. For instance, there are things that we know are good for us to do and there are things bad for us to do. I've looked on both sides, the devil's side, if you wish, whoever he may be, and with great zest.

PSYCHIC: What is this "other side" to you?

GARRETT: Well, there is a force in the universe available to everyone. One can use it for evil or for good. But one pays for one's actions, because there is a higher order that reveals us to ourselves. This I believe.

I had a great friend who sought nothing but evil and that was Aleister Crowley. He was an amazing, forceful man, a mountain climber and educated at Cambridge, I believe. The Great Beast, he called himself. He was one of those people who went the other way; he just laughed at his friends and used them for his own purposes. I think he grew terrified of himself; he'd done so much harm to so many people. In the end, he really couldn't live with himself. That I consider is using life for evil purposes.

PSYCHIC: Retribution is associated with evil in most religions, isn't it?

GARRETT: In a sense, yes. And most people eventually ask, "What have we lived for, why have we come?" Well, I think it's because there is a greater law than we can comprehend, which to me is the responsible law.

And I think most of the churches have lost this responsibility, because of the hypocrisy surrounding them—talking about the spiritual, on the one hand, and busy with the material, on the other. Even though, I have met many men of God doing great work in the church, and I have also met some real pilferers. Yet perhaps we're all hypocritical enough to need an altar some place.

PSYCHIC: Maybe this is the reason for the popular attention now given to Eastern philosophy and mysticism in the West.

GARRETT: While I haven't studied Eastern philosophy and mysticism, I can't help thinking that they know a great deal more about life and they have more responsibility for living, and so mysticism has come forth. We don't understand it, yet there remains this deep attitude toward it.

PSYCHIC: What is your opinion about the dimensions you have been able to tap in your subconscious?

GARRETT: I don't know about dimensions; rather, I think of the levels of experiences that I live through.

When I work, I deeply identify with the people for whom I work. I can't remain myself, you see. I must in a sense become a part of the other person, in order to know him. In doing this I get outside myself and become a part of that personality so that I become aware of the many difficulties and weaknesses. If I see something during the process where I think I can help, I mention it, and if I can't help, I leave it alone.

In my sittings, I believe that I am able through the aid of the controls—who may be split-offs of my own personality, how do I know?—to gain helpful information. However, I keep them at a distance and I stay within myself. But there are those with whom the controls or myself cannot identify. On the other hand, when I call upon them for significant help, they are willing to give advice.

PSYCHIC: Have you reached any conclusion about your controls?

GARRETT: No, and I still have a certain amount of awe for them. I don't know who they are; I don't know why they come. As I've said, they could be split-offs of my own personality, fragments of my *self*. I have left this question open in my own mind, and there it remains.

Oh, they have been asked what they think about my unyieldingness about them, but apparently they don't mind. They say they would rather have it this way. This has been recorded by Drs. Meyer, Brown, and Progoff, who have also done research on this aspect of my psychic abilities. I spent a great deal of time not too long ago with Dr. Progoff, a psychiatrist, who made a detailed analysis of my mediumship, published in his book *The Image of an Oracle*. I think Dr. Progoff is organizing an institute and will use his book about me as a text to some extent.

I also underwent analysis with Dr. Adolph Meyer, one of the great psychologists and psychiatrists of our day at Johns Hopkins University, to understand myself. His analysis was that the mind had made itself another channel and that channel had to be filled.

PSYCHIC: Is this what most analysts you have seen have concluded about your mediumship?

GARRETT: I think in general, yes, that I somehow have another channel to the subconscious or to other people's subconsciouses, but without any adverse affect on my own psyche.

I had also gone to see Carl Jung, the great Swiss psychologist and analyst, who in every sense of the word was a real master. I had great respect for Dr. Jung and all he stood for, so I got to know him rather well, having spent a good deal of time with him. He felt that I somehow had access to the far reaches of my own subconscious as well as the collective unconscious, a term which he used to describe

that vast, unexplained link between mind, nature, and the universe.
PSYCHIC: Then you've worked with both Freudians and Jungians?
GARRETT: Oh, yes. But I preferred the Freudians, because I knew on what level they were working. They also have much to say about sex. As far as I am concerned, sex is something I can use to produce, to create with, to transmute the energy into other channels. I can use sex energy in the process of healing and this is an important part of my life.
PSYCHIC: Do you think the field of parapsychology has progressed since your earlier works?
GARRETT: Yes, I think it has grown extensively. It has grown more popular, of course, but is now looked upon with greater respect than was given it fifty years ago.
PSYCHIC: What then do you think is needed to give impetus to the field?
GARRETT: Some good leadership. Several individuals in the field could have done so much more, including the scientific research organizations. But you have to know how to help people, how to open the door and let them in. When you set yourself up in any field, then you have to open yourself also to being helpful.
PSYCHIC: What do you see as parapsychology's future?
GARRETT: The young people are giving much more attention to the field of psychical research. I gather from the many scientists who attend conferences that deal with the subject of psychical research that parapsychology is gaining the attention and respect of many scientific disciplines and is making a place for itself in the world of science.

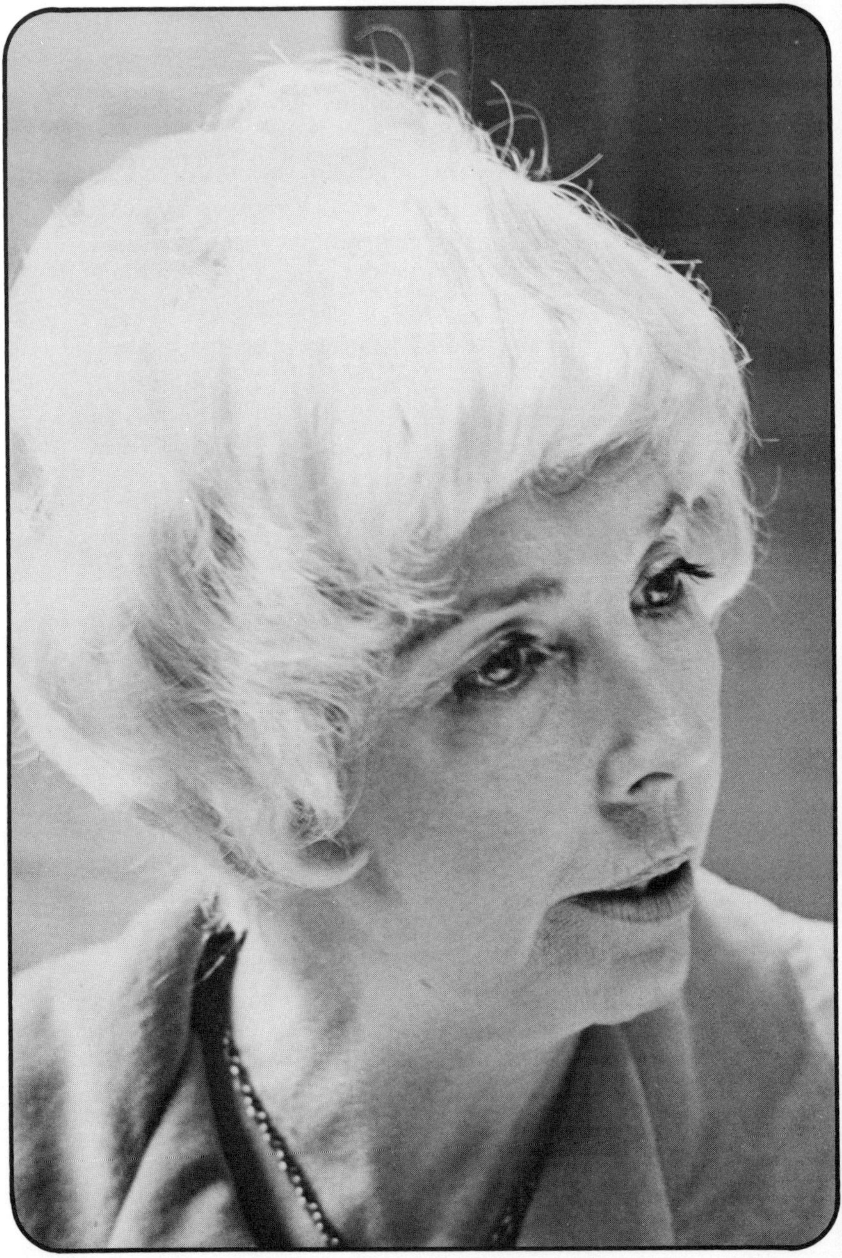

four
Irene F. Hughes

Born in a log cabin in Tennessee on farmland near the Mississippi border, Irene Finger Hughes grew up in a large family that tilled the soil for a living. Her parents, Joe and Easter Bell Finger, raised eleven children, of whom Irene was the eighth. Her mother was the daughter of a full-blooded Cherokee Indian woman, and seemed to possess psychic abilities which she used in "reading" coffee grounds. From her father's Scotch-Irish ancestry Mrs. Hughes inherited her blue eyes and blonde hair.

Mrs. Hughes's psychic gifts emerged as a child, and her mother assured her that being psychic was perfectly natural.

When her parents moved to Memphis, Mrs. Hughes, then fifteen, decided to join her sister in New Orleans, where she worked for five years in a hospital. During that time she was able to complete secretarial school and took a position with the president of the Louisiana Board of Medical Examiners.

In 1941 at an amusement park Mrs. Hughes urged her brother-in-law to introduce her to a soldier. His name was Bill Hughes. She had previously written down the name "Bill" as someone who would be important to her.

After Pearl Harbor, Bill Hughes was sent to the South Pacific, where he was wounded in combat by a bayonet. Mrs. Hughes saw the dread incident in a dream four months later as a telegram was on its way to Bill's sister with the news of his being wounded and convalescing in a hospital. The Hugheses were married in 1945 when he returned home. On their way to Chicago, the couple was marooned by a blizzard for three days, and nine months later their son Bill III was born.

Living near Chicago, the Hugheses had three more children, Karen, Patricia, and Kathleen while Mrs. Hughes was working as a reporter for the Calumet Index. Her zealousness as a reporter in exposing criminal activities resulted in personal threats which led to a forced sojourn in New Orleans. She was able to finance her return to Chicago by getting psychic impressions about the winners of horse races. Her husband, Bill, in the meanwhile, took a position with the Ford Motor Company, still his present employer.

For six years Mrs. Hughes worked as a secretary to an executive of an engineering publishing company. In 1961, shortly after a major operation, she first became aware (to her consternation) of a "spirit guide," a Japanese. She recounts how he made predictions for her future. Mrs. Hughes wondered if it were just a vivid dream. However, the "guide" gave her the name and address of his daughter, who, he said, was studying at Cornell University. From an inquiry, she received—to her surprise—an answer from the student and learned that the Japanese had died just two months before he appeared to the psychic.

In the years that followed, Irene F. Hughes established herself as a professional psychic, giving private consultations, lecturing, making predictions in her weekly syndicated newspaper column for

Community Publications, and recently authoring a syndicated astrology column. She was also editor for a medical publication, The International Journal of Neuropsychiatry, *which in 1966 featured an issue on parapsychology.*

In 1967 she visited the Physical Research Foundation in Durham, North Carolina, where she was tested for her psychic abilities by parapsychologist W. G. Roll. Roll's tests showed what Irene Hughes had known all along: she was psychic.

At her organization the Golden Path (30 W. Washington St., Chicago, Illinois 60602), founded in 1963, the midwestern seeress teaches classes in psychic subjects and tests students, hoping to develop their own psychic abilities.

Mrs. Hughes recently hosted her own television show for Chicago's WSNS and now frequently makes guest appearances on TV talk shows. Her life story and prophecies were the subject of a recent book by Brad Steiger, Know Your Future Today, *and she continues to make headlines with the fulfillment of her published predictions.*

PSYCHIC: How did you first become aware that you were psychic?
HUGHES: At four years old I had an experience that you might call psychic. I would talk to what appeared to be a fairy. But now I think it was a spirit that came to materialize. It was a very interesting experience.
PSYCHIC: Did this lead into any other psychic experience?
HUGHES: Yes, it seemed to me that when that happened I suddenly began to know too much. It was as though my whole head opened up—I knew everything that was going on with my older sisters and brothers. I would tell my mother when people were going to come home or when she was going to get a letter. It just seemed like suddenly everything came flooding in.
PSYCHIC: How did you develop your psychic ability?
HUGHES: Well it seemed to be just the thing that happened with me.

I'd never heard the word ESP at that time. The only thing I knew was that my mother read coffee grounds for herself and for my father, and once in a while for one of the children. So when this started happening to me she said, "It's all right. Everybody has these feelings. It's a natural thing."

PSYCHIC: Did she make predictions from coffee grounds?

HUGHES: Yes she did, and they were very accurate, too.

PSYCHIC: And how do you make your predictions?

HUGHES: My predictions, I feel, are made through many different ways. Through clairvoyance, if I'm having an experience of seeing a situation that is about to happen or will happen in the future.

I see a very clear mental image sometimes, just like watching a fast-moving movie, except it seems to me that I'm very close and an observer. Sometimes I feel I'm a participant in the action, even though it may not have anything to do with me, like an international situation. Then I do use psychometry when I'm working on police cases and I make predictions of what will happen based on that.

I know that I pick up thoughts by telepathy occasionally, but I can tell the difference, so that I don't make a prediction based on a thought unless I see clairvoyantly that it is going to happen. I am a trance medium, but I haven't done trance for quite a long while.

PSYCHIC: Do you have a spirit guide?

HUGHES: Yes. A Japanese, who appeared to me in 1961, made predictions which have come to pass.

PSYCHIC: What sort of things has he told you?

HUGHES: The first thing he told me was what would happen in my life and that I must be prepared for certain things. And then he began to show to me some tragedies that would happen in the space program.

PSYCHIC: What sort of tragedies?

HUGHES: He showed me three men dying in a space ship, which actually came about when three men died in an Apollo capsule fire in 1965. That prediction is on tape in Washington, D.C.

PSYCHIC: How about the Apollo 13, did you get a premonition about that mishap?

HUGHES: Yes, I did. About three days before the countdown I started dreaming all the situations that were going to happen to it. I called a friend in Washington who had been with NASA and I asked him to please tell the doctors at NASA to check out the astronauts because I felt they were becoming ill. I said that there would be a short in an electrical wire that would cause a problem like an explosion, and there would be an oil leakage. I said they would get toward the moon, but would not land on the moon yet they would get back to earth. This prediction was published, too, before it happened.
PSYCHIC: Didn't you have a premonition of John F. Kennedy's assassination?
HUGHES: Yes, that I wrote down in my shorthand notebooks in which I've written down predictions since I was fifteen. I indicated that he would be assassinated and that rifles would be used, more than one, and that it would be a conspiracy. I said that twenty-five years after it happened, the truth would be known—it would be terribly shocking to our nation to find out the people who were involved in that conspiracy, but they will never be brought to justice.
PSYCHIC: Did you attempt to warn President Kennedy or tell someone close to him?
HUGHES: No, I did not, because I feel I am never to interfere with a particular plan in a person's life. Therefore, I would not be allowed by the God force within me to reveal something if it interfered with that God plan. I feel that the true psychic not only gets the prediction, but he gets the information with it as to whether or not he should reveal it.
PSYCHIC: How about Robert Kennedy's assassination?
HUGHES: That was entirely different. I had a premonition when a newspaper reporter and I were coming back from investigating a haunted house in Monticello, Illinois. Suddenly she just asked out of the blue, "Well, what's going to happen to Bobby Kennedy?" And I said to her, "He's going to be shot through the head." She suddenly put on the brakes of the car and pulled over to the side of the road, and she said, "I'm shocked. I've got to go back and tell my managing editor." She told him, but he didn't put it in the paper.

Then Senator Harold Hughes (no relation), who was governor of Iowa at the time, asked for a reading, and in that reading Jack Kennedy appeared through my mediumistic ability and said, "Bobby's going to be here in six weeks. He's going to be shot through the head." He showed me then a scene of people around the eternal flame singing very sad songs. After it happened Governor Hughes wrote me a letter confirming that I had told him that in the reading.

PSYCHIC: Again, did you feel this was predestined, or that no warning would have made any difference?

HUGHES: In that case the governor did know about it, but I feel that if it is a person's destiny, nothing is going to change it. It was interesting that Robert was supposed to go through the ballroom and out one door, but at the last moment decided to turn around and go out through the kitchen way.

PSYCHIC: Have you had any other impressions about the Kennedy family?

HUGHES: Yes, I had an impression about Ted Kennedy's accident at Chappaquiddick. Bob Cummings, a Canadian radio personality, taped it and broadcast it June 9, 1969. My exact words were: "He will be involved in an auto accident on or near the water. His companion will be fatally injured, but he may not be injured."

I was introduced to Ted Kennedy in Washington and talked to him on June 30th before the accident happened on July 18th. He was very easy to talk to and expressed an interest in these things, but I really couldn't warn him because within me I was told not to tell him this, so the only thing I said in our conversation was that the month of July would be an accident-prone month for him.

PSYCHIC: How long have you been making predictions in print?

HUGHES: Since 1959. But I've had my regular column in thirty-two papers since 1966. In August 1966 I predicted the exact dates of the three blizzards in 1967. It was strange—I kept feeling as if I were in a snowstorm, yet it was hot weather in August. Then I saw the dates come one by one like numbers on a ticker tape.

PSYCHIC: What do you feel prophecy reveals about the concept of free will versus destiny?

HUGHES: My idea of free will is that the spirit or the soul as a cell of life makes its own destiny. It decides what it will do or what it has to do and therefore chooses the physical body in which it will live during life's experiences. The moment it enters into a physical body, it has already sacrificed free will because it used free will in creating its destiny in the beginning.

PSYCHIC: So you're saying, then, a person is born with an inner knowing of his future, or inner desire for certain events to take place?

HUGHES: I feel that he is born with the inner knowledge of his future, but it may take him years before he then becomes aware of that inner knowledge.

PSYCHIC: Do you feel the source of your psychic predictions is this inner knowledge?

HUGHES: I feel that each person has the mechanism within him—his soul—and also that the brain is like a radar system that can reach out into the universe and use magnetic currents to bring in the life history of a particular person or nation or whatever. And then the brain creates images to impress upon the psychic the exactness of the situation.

PSYCHIC: So your concept would be that events already exist in the future?

HUGHES: Yes. I feel the whole picture is already here. That everything that ever was or ever will be is already in this universe in some form and that the more sensitive a person is, the more easily he can bring this into the picture.

PSYCHIC: Do you think a person can do this by himself?

HUGHES: I feel that I can. I do get impressions about my own future. And I feel it is possible that other people can.

PSYCHIC: Have you ever met Jeane Dixon?

HUGHES: Yes. I met Jeane Dixon about eight years ago. We had a very good conference together and discussed many international things and things about her life. I gave her a pretty good reading about certain things that were going to happen to her, such as her children-to-children project.

PSYCHIC: Did you find you had both simultaneously come up with the same prediction, but independently?

HUGHES: Yes, and I think that this happens to many psychics. Sometimes their predictions are the same—they use almost the same words—and they may not even know each other. This is an indication that perhaps telepathic communication works in those cases.

PSYCHIC: What do you think accounts for that?

HUGHES: I feel that the answer is revealed to each individual in the way in which we can receive it and also that different psychics use different abilities.

PSYCHIC: What do you think accounts for prophecies that are not fulfilled?

HUGHES: In those cases, I know beyond doubt that the psychic sees or feels or senses the situation involving the prediction, but may not have time enough to see all the prediction psychically, and he predicts on what is seen. Or, it is very possible that the feeling indicating whether it will or will not happen may not have been strong enough.

I know, as far as I am concerned, that I misinterpreted certain symbols in certain predictions, and missed. Also I have missed on the *time level* involving predictions, but it seems that if I do miss—even a year's time level—the predictions, do happen. I have, for instance, misinterpreted the figure five as five months when it was actually five years.

Time is extremely difficult for the psychic to interpret. I feel that if all predictions made by psychics were checked out years later, people would be astounded to find that they did happen.

PSYCHIC: Do you feel that your own opinions about things ever influence or color your predictions?

HUGHES: Only once that I know of did I allow my own feeling to color a prediction. It was one I made about Senator Douglas and Senator Percy, both of Illinois. I knew Senator Douglas's background and respected him and felt he should have the opportunity of staying in office.

However, it's interesting how I published that prediction: "I predict that Senator Douglas will win but every time I say that, I see Senator Percy's hand go up in victory." Of course, Percy won.

PSYCHIC: Do you think there is anything the ordinary person can do in response to things that are coming?

HUGHES: I feel that each individual can try to prepare himself or herself psychologically and by becoming more aware of his spiritual gifts.

PSYCHIC: Do you think it's possible that some disasters could be averted by warnings from psychics?

HUGHES: Absolutely! Many can be. This is why prophecy was used in the old days to warn nations about other nations invading them, and what they should do. So I feel that it certainly can be very valuable in preventing tragedies and accidents from happening even down to the individual's personal life.

PSYCHIC: Do you think the Central Premonitions Registry's (Box 482, New York, New York 10036) collecting of these premonitions could be of service?

HUGHES: Yes, I feel that could be very valuable to the nation. And I feel there will be tremendous opportunity for expansion there. I have started filing my predictions with them.

PSYCHIC: What about prophecy? Do you think it is a talent that anyone can develop?

HUGHES: I do not believe that every person has the ability to prophesy. Some people who have the ability of seeing things psychially are able to make predictions. There are people who have the gift of healing and who cannot prophesy. There are even people who have precognitive dreams who cannot prophesy. I believe that each individual has his own ability and that not all people have the same abilities.

PSYCHIC: But you say prophecy comes to you in dreams, in trance, and in waking states.

HUGHES: Yes, in the waking state it is like a "daylight" trance. And I have made some predictions working through psychometry, just by holding an object. This to me is one of the most unusual areas of work that I do. How can I know what's going to happen five or ten years into the future of a person just by holding his watch?

PSYCHIC: Do you think by holding a person's watch you're tuning into the person rather than getting the future from the watch?

HUGHES: Well, no. Just by touching something we stamp our life plan on it, and when the psychic touches it, then this magnetic-like energy leads the psychic into time. I feel in the future we will determine to a very great extent exactly how these things work, and that electromagnetic currents have much to do with it.

PSYCHIC: Do you ever get feelings of discarnates' presence?

HUGHES: Oh yes. Even in my counseling sessions, which only last half an hour, and I am in a light trance. Often I bring forth those who've passed on to my sitters. And most people accept it.

PSYCHIC: Do you feel there's a difference between the way you perceive the information about those who are alive and those who are dead?

HUGHES: I've studied myself all these years—the way that these abilities have been working through me—and I have some theories of my own. I feel that electromagnetic currents are very much involved and that a dead person's thoughts are energy that remains in the universe. When their thoughts begin to come through about the person who is sitting before me, then automatically a mental image of them appears, created by those electromagnetic currents.

PSYCHIC: Didn't you pick up something about Bishop Pike?

HUGHES: Yes, I did. I was asked to participate in a workshop at the Spiritual Frontiers Convention in 1970 on the same program with Diane Pike. During our workshop I asked her to answer a question that had been directed to me and as I stepped back away from the microphone I felt the presence of the bishop. He said to me that he was having most unusual headaches about three days before they went into the wilderness. And it seemed this related to some very important incident.

And so I told Diane and she admitted that this was true, and only she and a relative knew about it. She felt that was highly evidential.

PSYCHIC: Do you believe that survival in any way conflicts with the idea of reincarnation?

HUGHES: No, I do not. I believe that survival of the spirit after death very definitely confirms reincarnation, because there must be spirit like that to reincarnate into another physical body.

PSYCHIC: Have you ever had any psychic impressions about other people's former lives or future lives?

HUGHES: Yes. Something about former lives now and then slips through. One man came to me and wanted to know who he would be in his next life so he could leave all his money to himself. I didn't see who he was going to be, so I told him he'd have to seek another psychic who had capabilities I don't have.

Once in a while I can see a flash of what a person has been. But since I've got into astrology I feel there are different ways of telling through astrology of where and who a person might have been.

When I was a child I caused my mother a lot of pain because I'd say to her, "Gee, that person is an old crab or that person looks like a bull and acts like a bull." I applied animal symbols like that to every person. My mother would say to me, "Why?" And I would say, "Because I see it above their head." Later I found out these are the astrology symbols. I didn't know anything about it then.

PSYCHIC: Do you think astrology is a science or does it have to be interpreted by a psychic?

HUGHES: I feel astrology is a science. But I feel that I as a psychic can go beyond just the knowledge learned from books about astrology and can perhaps do deeper interpretations.

PSYCHIC: Have you had any experience with psychokinesis?

HUGHES: I remember an incident that happened when I was working with the managing editor of a magazine. We were having a pretty heated up day. You know how it can get with publishing. She said something and I said, "Now that you've made me ruin this, I've got to throw it in the wastebasket. I'm sick and tired of getting up from my desk and walking over to the wastebasket. Come over to me wastebasket." She was standing there with her mouth wide open because I'd never thrown a tantrum like that. And do you know the wastebasket moved. We both became very frightened. I threw the paper in it and said, "Never again."

PSYCHIC: Have you ever had any experiences with psychic healing?

HUGHES: I do work with healing through the laying on of hands and

through thought projection. I have had very good results.
PSYCHIC: Do you work with doctors on this?
HUGHES: I did work with a psychiatrist for a while. He carried on some experiments with me, too. And a doctor once asked me to read some X-rays and I explained to him what I felt was wrong with the person, which he confirmed, and I also correctly told him the date the person was going to die.
PSYCHIC: What about your work with the police?
HUGHES: I have worked on many cases. Once a police captain called me into the office and asked me to work on a murder case. The sergeant brought up a box and took a human skull out of it. He put it in my hands and said in a gruff voice, "What do you get from that?" I answered, "A heart attack." And then I told him the name of the person who had been murdered, and it was his turn almost to have a heart attack. I indicated the name of a place where I felt that the murders were contemplated. The police did find a place by that name and found that it was where the murderer contemplated the first of five murders.

I feel there will eventually be a crime laboratory composed of psychics, and there may be a whole psychic force in the future working with the police. I really feel the police are going to be far more open to this than they have been.
PSYCHIC: How did the Canadians make use of your prediction about the LaPorte-Cross kidnapings?
HUGHES: Bob Cummings, a Canadian radio announcer, telephoned me and tape-recorded my impressions about the kidnap victims. I described the house in which Mr. Cross was being detained, and how he could go free. I said that Mr. LaPorte would be assassinated. I told him a name connected with the case and I predicted the exact day on which the arrest would be made. I have no written proof that the Canadian Government used my impressions, but I know as a psychic that they did. But I didn't get the fifty-thousand-dollar reward, so maybe they'll read this and do something about the reward.
PSYCHIC: If you had fifty-thousand dollars, what would you do with it?

HUGHES: I would immediately start the building of a spiritual retreat. I would need dormitories for men and women, classrooms, and so on.

My other goal is to establish a university of parapsychology where scientists from all over the world can gather together and work strictly in the field of parapsychology without being hampered by lack of finances.

PSYCHIC: What sort of work have you done with parapsychologists?

HUGHES: William Roll invited me to Durham [North Carolina] for testing at his Psychical Research Foundation. In the week I was there he put me through many different tests to determine whether or not I had psychic abilities. One of the tests was with an identi-kit obtained from the police. I would assemble the features of persons brought into another room of the laboratory.

And then I had a complete psychiatric examination. That was a lot of fun because the psychiatrists were afraid that I would know everything that they were going to do.

However, I feel that parapsychologists really should go back to the old methods of sitting with mediums week after week and let their abilities be used in a natural way rather than using superficial methods of testing. The statistical methods are fine, but they may not really prove the person's real abilities. I feel that parapsychologists could determine better how ESP operates if they worked with a person more closely.

PSYCHIC: Do you have any feelings about the future of parapsychology?

HUGHES: Yes. I think that parapsychology will really bloom forth for the next hundred years. It will be the Age of the Mind—the expansion of man's consciousness and the mystical side of life.

I also predicted that psychiatry would change totally and would merge with parapsychology. Psychiatrists will become more deeply involved in the investigation of the mind with parapsychologists.

PSYCHIC: Do you think psychic phenomena today have spiritual implications?

HUGHES: I certainly do, yes. And I feel in the future that they will have greater spiritual implications because more people will realize that religion had its foundation in mystical or spiritual experiences—so they're one and the same.

PSYCHIC: What is your philosophy of life?

HUGHES: I feel that regardless of whether a person travels the rocky road of poverty, physical despair, or anguish or whether he travels the very smooth road of material success and social status, that each person will come to the same conclusion finally in spiritual awareness. People are going to realize that material things are not everything and they'll begin to focus on the spiritual and become more aware of the God-consciousness within them.

PSYCHIC: How do you conceive of God?

HUGHES: I feel that there are as many definitions of God as there are people in the world. I feel that maybe God is an energy—a spirit—that energy and spirit of love and healing that is all around us and that keeps everything in its proper place. And because God is all and everywhere, it is the original source, I believe, of everything. As man becomes more spiritually aware, small groups will gather together to realize the truth of God within man.

PSYCHIC: Do you think this will take the place of organized religion?

HUGHES: Yes. I feel that it will and I feel that it's not going to bring any heartbreak to people. I feel they are going to enjoy it. As we near the ending of this civilization and the beginning of a new civilization, our philosophies and religious beliefs will come to an end, and new ones will be toddling to the fore.

PSYCHIC: Do you associate this with the Age of Aquarius?

HUGHES: I feel that this is before the Age of Aquarius, that we are in the final stage of what we call astrologically the Piscean Age. But regardless of the astrological age, I feel it is the age of expansion of man's consciousness—of tremendous exploration of his mind and brain.

PSYCHIC: Do you think this will be beneficial to man in his ordinary life?

HUGHES: Yes, I do. I feel that man can use his psychic abilities in his everyday life. In the business field, for instance, a man who may wish to sell someone something would first tune into that person and realize whether or not the sale would go through. If it appeared to him that it would not go through, he would not waste his time and effort, but instead go to another person.

And also I feel that when people are in a position where other people owe them money—even doctors or lawyers who have clients who owe them money—that what they should do is to sit down and to try to visualize that person being blessed with prosperity so that they'll have enough money to come and pay them. They can work for their own good and use their knowledge of the mystical to help themselves.

PSYCHIC: Do you think it is possible to bring conditions into being by visualizing them?

HUGHES: I feel that conditions are already there and that we can approach the right moment to do it, and that those who do not know can be taught to do it. We are cameras, and when we focus properly and use proper development methods, we can do it.

PSYCHIC: What do you think are some possibilities for conditions in the future?

HUGHES: It is my psychic impression that there are going to be unbelievable breakthroughs in many areas of what we call older diseases such as arthritis, multiple sclerosis, and epilepsy, throughout the 1970s and 1980s. Actually, I feel that there is an urgency in this research because there will be other, new diseases appearing that research will have to be done on.

In the educational field, I long ago saw machines that would be used in teaching. Now I have come to the conclusion that these will be called computer data centers and that they will be established in the community where students can go and sit in a little machine and actually visualize subjects on a screen. There will be fewer subjects taught. The student will be oriented more toward life and living than just going on to higher education as he has in the past.

For television I see the most fantastic breakthrough that will happen in the next three to five years with total education for the elementary grades going on television, so that the tiny tots up through grade six can study at home and actually be graded.

By the year 1982 I foresee that a new monetary system for the United States will come into being. The new economic structure will be a much simpler system, but the United States will not be the only country that will undergo a complete change of its financial order. Many nations will enter into a cooperative structure that will lead to a world monetary system. How easy it will then be to travel—no cash, no checks, just a card to symbolize money.

By the year 2026 the United States Constitution, as we know it, will be no more. In its place will be an entirely different document and an entirely new method of governmental rule. Long before that year, I foresee machines that will receive and process legal complaints, and I can envision the need for extensive laws passing from man's existence.

In 2026, man will be much happier than he is today, and he will have more freedom in all areas of life. Man will live in greater trust and in greater love of his fellow man at that time than at any other era of history.

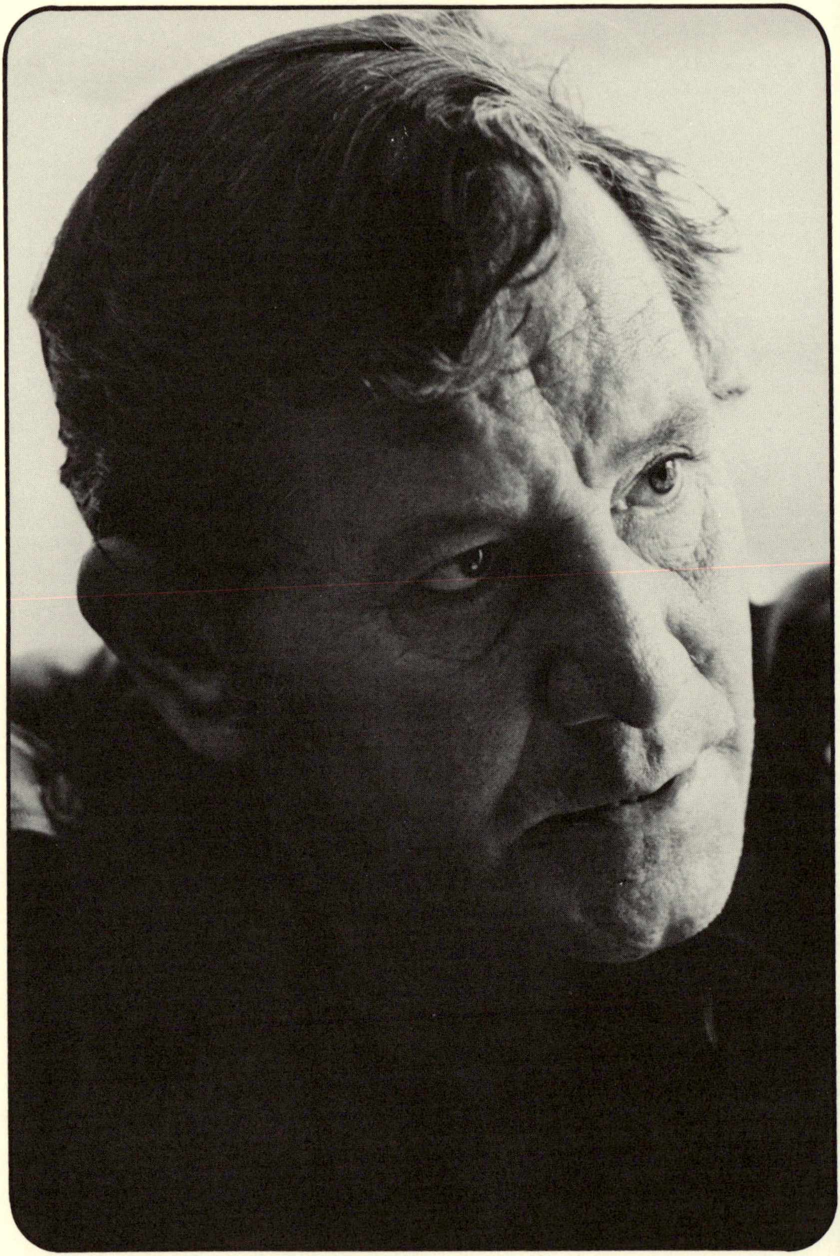

five
Peter Hurkos

Peter Hurkos was born Pieter Van der Hurk on May 21, 1911, in Dordrecht, Holland, a small town about twenty miles from The Hague.

His father, a native of Holland, was a small painting contractor there, though he has since retired and now lives with his son in America. His mother, a meticulous Dutch housewife and also a native of Holland, died some years ago. Besides Peter, there is an older brother, Niko, and two younger sisters, Ali and Willi.

Young Peter was schooled in his native Dordrecht, where he completed his public education. He later entered a technical school—equivalent to a combined high school and college in America—but was forced to leave after two years owing to lack of funds and because his father needed him in the family's painting business. That was in 1926 when he was sixteen.

Shortly after, he became a merchant seaman, alternating for a while between helping his father in summers and shipping out to sea in winters.

When his job as a sailor became a full-time career, he began working his way up through the ranks and eventually was offered a position as a talleyman in Shanghai—checking cargo and passengers.

In 1939, after four years in Shanghai, war broke out in the Far East disrupting shipping and subsequently his job. He returned home.

By 1940, the war clouds had settled over Holland. The Netherlands soon fell, the government surrendering after heavy German bombing attacks.

Like most young Dutchmen, Pieter Van der Hurk joined the newly organized underground to fight against the Germans. It was then that he changed his name to Hurkos, to protect his family against possible reprisals.

During the occupation, he worked at odd jobs for the Germans, thwarting their war efforts whenever possible through sabotage and espionage. In addition, he helped steal weapons, munitions, and other materials for use in the resistance.

But as a member of the underground, he was forced to jump from job to job to avoid detection, which included brief periods of working for his father. It was while helping his father paint houses in 1941 that an accident occurred which nearly cost him his life and which resulted in his psychic ability manifesting itself. He fell thirty-six feet from a ladder, landing on his head and shoulder.

For three days he lay unconscious in a hospital, but subsequently came to, only to discover a new but perplexing ability: he could pick up information about people and things merely by touching them.

After being released from the hospital, Hurkos returned to work and his double life in the underground. Toward war's end, however, he was caught with forged papers and shipped to internment at Buchenwald in Germany. Liberation came shortly after D-Day, when American and Canadian troops overran the infamous prison camp, setting its surviving occupants free. Once back home and recuperated, Peter Hurkos discovered he could no longer work at past familiar jobs—his psychic ability was too distracting.

It wasn't long before people began to learn of Peter Hurkos's unusual ability and started to request his appearance before groups. By 1946 he was helping with church benefits, later accepting theatrical bookings. His popular performances led to a tour of Europe, and he has been appearing on stage and television off and on ever since.

During his psychic life, Peter Hurkos has also helped police departments throughout the world—in countries such as England, France, Germany, Belgium, his native Holland, and the United States.

He was brought to this country in 1956 by Andrija Puharich, M.D., then director of the Round Table Foundation in Glen Cove, Maine, which had a complete laboratory for conducting psychical research. There Hurkos was tested for two and a half years under Dr. Puharich's direction. The results were published in Dr. Puharich's books, The Sacred Mushroom and Beyond Telepathy.

Over the years Peter Hurkos has received recognition for his psychic as well nonpsychic work from distinguished people around the world, including the late Pope Pius XII and Queen Juliana of Holland. He also holds several honorary badges from police departments in this country, and a card from the Union des Anciens Combattants de le Prefecture de Police in Paris.

Today, Peter Hurkos appears throughout the country on television shows, in theaters, and at special gatherings, benefits, and an occasional police department.

PSYCHIC: What psychic abilities do you have?
HURKOS: I'm a psychometrist. I can touch things and then tell you

what I see—information about them that just comes to me. Sometimes it's past, sometimes the present, and sometimes the future.

In scientific terminology it's called psychometrics—touching objects or people and obtaining information about them. But I don't always have to touch them, though it works better if I do.

PSYCHIC: How long have you been able to do this?

HURKOS: About twenty-nine years now. It all started in Holland, from a fall that nearly killed me. I was painting a house and fell thirty-six feet from a ladder. The fall left me with a bad concussion and a broken shoulder. I think if I hadn't partially landed on my shoulder I would have died. I was unconscious for three days in the hospital. Today my left shoulder is lower than my right one because of this, and I have a bump on the back of my head, too.

PSYCHIC: Were you psychic before your fall?

HURKOS: No. And after I came to and started to recover I was very upset about this strange feeling and ability to pick up information about people and things. I didn't know what to do with it.

The doctors were puzzled, too. Even a psychiatrist worked with me and tested me. Since the doctors had no idea what caused it, or could do anything to take it away, I gradually had to learn to live with it. They still have no idea what causes it, despite many tests, X-rays, and medical examinations.

PSYCHIC: Was anyone in your family psychic?

HURKOS: My mother was. She would read cards for people, but not for money. She told me one time, when I was about twenty, that I would be well-known some day. I asked her, "As a sailor?" She said she didn't know, but that I would not die in my own country, but in a big country where they speak English. And I laughed.

As I look back, I don't think she actually "read" the cards, she just used them. But when I was a sailor, I didn't believe her at all. And, of course, she often got mad at me for this.

PSYCHIC: What kind of impressions do you receive when you touch an object?

HURKOS: That's very difficult to say. But it's like a movie. And I have to forget my private life, my family life. I have to blank everything out. Then I get this feeling and somehow make mental pictures, like a television picture.

If I'm emotionally upset, though, I'm not worth a dime. Or when people tell me things about themselves, I become confused. The best way is not to tell me anything, that's when I get my best results.

PSYCHIC: How are you able to make your mind blank?

HURKOS: I've always been able to concentrate on things for long periods of time. People could say something to me and it wouldn't even register. I suppose it's similar to meditation.

PSYCHIC: Are you ever bombarded by a lot of extraneous impressions so that you have to seclude yourself from people to rest?

HURKOS: Sometimes, when I work on television. I'm usually given one object right after another. Now this tires me—to break one contact and try to immediately pick up another one. In the beginning I had to wait five to ten minutes to get the first object out of my mind. But Dr. Puharich helped me to develop this ability—to forget the object and go right to another one.

PSYCHIC: Do you hear information as well as see it?

HURKOS: Yes, sometimes—names. It's like a sound wave. I don't know how to explain it.

PSYCHIC: Is it like a voice from outside, or does it come from within?

HURKOS: From outside, like someone speaking, only different. It's hard to explain.

PSYCHIC: Are you able to control your gift or does it come at random?

HURKOS: It's always there; I can do it any time. But I would be the most happy man in the world if I could switch it off for eight hours. It's always there, day and night.

PSYCHIC: Have you worked in scientific experiments?

HURKOS: Yes. I spent about two and a half years around 1956 with Dr. Andrija Puharich in his medical laboratory. He tested me on many things. In one experiment I was placed in a copper cage with high voltage electricity going through it [a faraday cage which screens out electromagnetic transmissions]. I remember how scared I was to get in that cage with all that voltage around it. It got tremendously hot inside during the experiments, and the high voltage prevented fresh air from circulating to us. We also had a candle burning inside to generate negative ions to offset the positive ions from the high voltage. We could only stay in the cage about an hour and a half.

Dr. Puharich tested my psychic ability inside the cage and other things that might require telepathy to see if the electromagnetic field had any effect.

It was strange, too, when I would come out after each test, I couldn't see color. Everything would be one color, it was dirty. And there was one time when I got rid of my asthma—after being in the cage for a long time. We never did know what caused that.

PSYCHIC: What other kinds of experiments did you do with Dr. Puharich?

HURKOS: Well, he would put objects in boxes and ask me to identify the contents. Sometimes he wouldn't let me touch the box to see if I could get information this way. I often got mad at him, too, because he wouldn't let me touch the box. Of course he wanted to see if I could do it without touching. But I didn't understand that at first. He was the one who discovered through these experiments that I could get information without having to touch an object—he developed me in this method; I didn't know I could do it.

He also tested me with pictures in envelopes. I remember one test when I picked up something about a child, a funny little guy. I could see him standing there and his humor-type character. I felt he was a child many years ago. Dr. Puharich asked me if he was still alive, and I didn't know. When he opened the envelope, it was a picture of Jackie Gleason as a child.

I also did a lot of testing with medical blood spots from animals and humans. I was very strong in this field, too—strong in finding people.

Dr. Puharich showed me I could do a lot more than I thought I could. But in the beginning I would say, "No, I must be wrong, it doesn't seem possible." I was confused and unsure. That's over. Now when I hit, I catch it and know it.

PSYCHIC: Do you think your gift has developed over the years?

HURKOS: No, it's the same as it's always been. I understand it more now and I'm more sure of myself.

I'm not afraid to be on television or to do tests scientists make up for me. In the beginning I worried, I didn't know what to do. Not now.

PSYCHIC: You have become well known as a psychic detective. Why have you become involved in trying to help police solve unsolved crimes?

HURKOS: It started when I was in Holland. I was asked to help locate a little girl who was missing. It was sad; some woman had killed her and threw her in the water. I found the girl's body and helped solve the case.

The next case concerned the coronation stone in England, the one stolen from the Abbey. This is when Scotland Yard in England called me through the police in Holland. I helped them with that case, too. From these and other cases, police departments have contacted me from time to time to help them.

PSYCHIC: Do you receive any money for this?

HURKOS: No, only my expenses are paid; that's all.

PSYCHIC: Do you have to prove your ability each time?

HURKOS: Usually, yes. But not with the ones I have worked with previously and who know me. And when I go into a new area, I always work with the police and never behind their backs.

But there is always skepticism when a psychic works with the police—he has to prove that he has the gift. For example, I usually ask them to take out a file on anybody and keep it closed. Then I tell them about it. This usually is proof enough. But unless I convince all of those working on the case that I can help, there is little cooperation and also the feeling that I am wasting their time.

I think it's strange that most policemen will take tips from practically anybody, but when a psychic comes along, he has to prove to them first that he can help—that he has the gift.

PSYCHIC: What are some of the cases you've worked on?

HURKOS: Once when I was in Palm Springs the chief of police called about his friend, a pilot, who was missing on a flight. I told him I would need some personal object from his friend's belongings, like clothing. The chief called the Air Force base outside of San Diego, and the base sent up clothing from one of the pilots.

When I got the clothing I asked for a map of the general area they were flying in and began getting information about what happened. I sensed the plane was off course, and I saw an explosion. I saw only two people in the plane and one out of the plane—all dead. Nine hours later they found the plane where I said they would—I was a mile off in an area of six hundred miles.

Then there was the time the Citizens Committee in Detroit invited me to help on the Ann Arbor coed case, where six girls were murdered. There were no clues or fingerprints. When I arrived they met me and we later drove out to where one of the girls was killed about a year and a half previously. It was a test to see what I could come up with. I located the place where the body had been found and in what position they found her.

Later, I went on television in Detroit, describing the murderer, who I felt had a trailer and a motor bike, and giving what I thought was his name. About two days later I received a threatening telephone call to get out of town.

The case was solved when the murderer's uncle found one of the victim's blood-stained pieces of clothing in his basement. His nephew had been staying there while he was gone. The uncle called the police, who picked the young man up. He did have a trailer, too, which was found in California.

PSYCHIC: Do you work with other psychics?

HURKOS: No. But one of the best psychics I ever met is Mary Pickford. Several years ago she told me that I was going to Vietnam to work for the State Department. I told her I was too old for that. But about two weeks later I was asked to go to Vietnam on the Thompson kidnaping case at the request of James Douglas, former Assistant Secretary of State under the Eisenhower administration. [James Thompson, a millionaire silk merchant in Southeast Asia, was believed captured by the communists in late 1967. He is still missing.]

PSYCHIC: Do you believe that if you misuse your gift you will lose it?

HURKOS: Maybe yes; maybe no. But I don't think so, although I do think I would get my punishment, if I misused it. I can use it in a good way or in a very bad way though. I have files on many people. If I were a bad person, I could easily blackmail them. But I have to live with myself. Besides, I think it is a gift to help others.

I must say, though, that in the beginning, when I was young, I unintentionally hurt many people—that was about twenty-eight years ago. For example, I said things that I shouldn't have said in front of other people—personal things that came out spontaneously. Later I realized, "My gosh, I shouldn't have said that." So finally, I learned to think about what I said before I said it; to make sure I didn't embarrass or hurt people. That's not what I want to do.

PSYCHIC: Can you apply your psychic gift to yourself—pick up your own past, present, or future?

HURKOS: Sometimes I can't even find my own shoes! No, I can't get anything directly about myself. But I'm glad I don't, because I probably wouldn't be able to sleep. This is funny isn't it? I can find missing people, but I can't find my shoes.

But there are times I can sense danger to myself. For instance, I never go on a plane unless I touch someone going on, too. I can pick up danger this way, if there is any. Also, when I see a person boarding a plane who no longer has color—who is blacked out—I won't go on the plane.

When I was in Bangkok, while working on the Thompson case, I was at the airport waiting to pass customs and a plane landed for a rest and refueling stop. I got to talking with one of the passengers, a German attorney. When I looked out at the plane later, it was completely black—no color. Since this means danger to me, I said to the attorney, "Why don't you wait for another plane, I don't think that one is going to make it." But he said he had to go, and he did. The next morning we read in the paper that the plane had crashed in the mountains.

I have tried to warn many people when I sense danger on occasions like this, but they usually don't believe me—they won't listen.

You see, everyone needs proof; and sometimes when proof comes, it is too late. But I do what I can at the time.

PSYCHIC: What do you think is the reason for your psychic ability?

HURKOS: I think it's a gift from God. I believe in God very strongly now, too, although before my gift I didn't believe in anything. I never went to church, either.

PSYCHIC: Since you believe in God, how do you see Him?

HURKOS: That's difficult to answer, because I really don't have a definite concept of God, yet I know He exists. Nevertheless, I think God gave me my gift just as He gives people various gifts—power over music, medicine, and many talents.

PSYCHIC: What then do you think is the purpose of life?

HURKOS: I believe that life is a test, that the world is a test to learn how to help others and to live with them in a good way. And I would say that the hell everybody talks about is right here. People don't understand each other; they kill one another. They are not satisfied in this world. I don't think, according to the Bible, that if you don't believe in God you go to hell. That's not right. You can't read the Bible like a book, because it's written in symbology—with a lot of psychic phenomena.

And I believe in reincarnation, too. And why are some children born blind, or a responsible man killed who has a lot of children to care for? It doesn't make sense that these people are given just one chance, or that this happens without some purpose. So you see, this is the hell, this is the test. You come back so many times to this world before you go on. There are many planes where others live—much higher and more aloft in understanding than this world. This is the test, where we live right now. And that's my philosophy.

PSYCHIC: Then you believe in other dimensions and existences. What kind?

HURKOS: I cannot answer that, but as I said, I believe that this world is the test before we go on. And if I didn't believe in reincarnation, I wouldn't believe in God.

This explains to me why you can be a very honest man, very simple, and still get hurt. People love to hurt each other. There are those who kill children for no reason, and now there are people killed in Vietnam. And why do we destroy food when so many are starving, just because the price isn't right—we dump it in the ocean?

Why doesn't God stop all of this? Well, I think He leaves this world as a test for us, where we learn how to treat others in the right way and live in harmony.

PSYCHIC: Have you ever experimented with psychedelic drugs in scientific experiments?

HURKOS: Yes, with Dr. Puharich. We experimented with the sacred mushroom, but only under medical control. I am very much against the use of drugs, especially LSD. People today use it for kicks, without any concern or knowledge how it will affect them. Some get panicky and cry, others want to kill, some want to go to heaven and talk to God—a hallucination.

PSYCHIC: Do you think there's any correlation between what happens under drugs and what happens in the mind with psychic powers?

HURKOS: That's hard to say. But a psychic doesn't need drugs, only to do experiments with.

For example, once when Dr. Puharich and I were experimenting with the sacred mushroom, I took it and was completely out—nobody could talk to me and I sat and stared for hours. After a while, Dr. Puharich finally got my attention and pulled out a letter from his desk, asking me to tell him about it.

Suddenly I was off to Chicago, as though flying through the air, above the city, and I described a house with a big picture in it and the man who wrote the letter—gray-haired and in his seventies. I could see the house where the letter came from.

PSYCHIC: That sounds like an out-of-the-body experience. Have you had others?

HURKOS: One other that I can remember. This was also with Dr. Puharich, when I was very tired after a hard day of work. I lay down to rest and fell right asleep. The next thing I knew I was standing by the door and saw myself lying in bed—my own body, living and breathing. I was away from my body and it was not a joke.

It's the only experience I had like this, and it wasn't a hallucination, because I felt clearly awake. Perhaps it was the result of overwork, I don't know.

PSYCHIC: Why have you pursued a career in the entertainment world?

HURKOS: I want to get through to all the people, and this is the best way I know how. Also, I have to eat. I can't go to the store and say, "Hello, I'm Peter Hurkos; I need some groceries." I have to pay. So I work with my gift to earn my living.

Besides, I was a guinea pig for a while and that doesn't offer much to live on.

PSYCHIC: How has your psychic ability affected your life?

HURKOS: As I've said, I had to adjust to it—very difficult at first. Then I have learned to live with picking up information about people and things—particularly in large gatherings—that I don't want to know. I don't want to know some of the personal things I pick up—it bothers me.

Also, I receive a lot of invitations from people to attend prominent parties and dinners; they would like a demonstration. But I try to steer clear of these now, since it's very exhausting and not very much fun or entertaining for me.

Even in Las Vegas it is different for me. Once I was there and played roulette. I told several people what the next number was going to be and we won. After this happened a few times the manager introduced himself and wanted to know how I did it. I said I was just lucky. When he learned who I was, though, he gave me a credit card to use on the house, but I had to promise not to gamble.

The word went down the strip and when I went to other casinos, I would be greeted by a man who would say, "Good evening, Mr. Hurkos, no gambling."

Now when I do a show in Las Vegas, there is a clause in the contract which prohibits me from gambling.

PSYCHIC: How do you think ESP is going to benefit man?

HURKOS: He will become more aware. He will learn to pay attention to his psychic ability—to his intuition—to help him in life, to live a better life and live in harmony with others.

And people will begin to realize that there is more to man than just the material things we see. That there is a part that needs understanding and developing in order to progress beyond just money, cars, and washing machines. You see, we have all of these luxuries and still we aren't satisfied.

Also, people will begin to realize there is a God and that you need faith beyond this life, because the hell you make is right here. So you have to keep coming back until you learn the right way.

I also think that the interest in psychic phenomena will continue to grow and that more and more people will want to know about it —try to understand it. And I wish the government would set up foundations and do research in psychic phenomena, because I believe everything is in the mind—the answers are there.

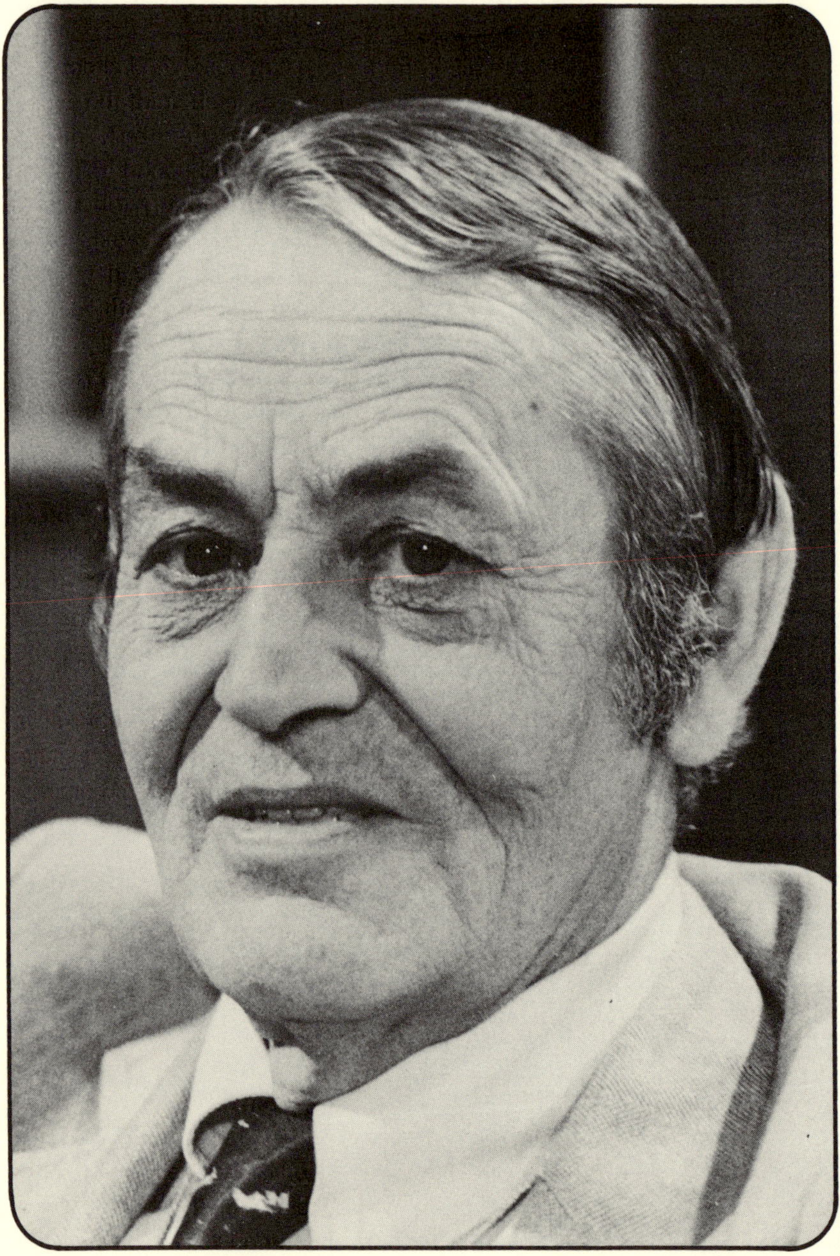

SIX
Douglas Johnson

Born in London before World War I, Douglas Johnson came from a family in "comfortable circumstances" and one that accepted psychic phenomena without fuss. His father, Francis, was a successful civil engineer, and his mother, Gladys, was a housewife. The most psychic member of the family was an aunt who was a medium. She predicted that one day young Douglas would become a famous psychic.

While still a young teenager, Johnson lost both his parents. A friend of his parents then brought him up.

On school holidays, young Douglas would attend a psychic development circle at the home of friends of his parents. One night, when he was fifteen, he fell unexpectedly into trance in the stuffy séance room. That was the first appearance of Johnson's trance personality called "Chiang," who claimed to have lived in China seven centuries ago. This experience thoroughly frightened young Johnson and "Chiang" did not appear again until many years later.

After finishing school, Johnson appeared briefly as an actor on the London stage before enlisting in the Royal Air Force, in which he served during World War II. While abroad, he was in contact with the College of Psychic Science in London, which furnished him with books on psychic subjects.

When the war ended, he returned to England and worked for a while in the office of a plastics firm. But in 1947, at the urging of the College of Psychic Science, he began giving trial sittings, and before long was established as a professional medium. In addition to the trance personality "Chiang," he acquired another control called "Zola," who claims to be a North African girl helping with survival communications.

Over the years, however, he has come to do most of his psychic work in a waking state. In 1960 he appeared on British television in a series of programs conducted by Dr. David Stafford-Clark. This was the first scientifically conducted test of a medium on television.

Johnson did a number of experiments for the Society for Psychical Research in London and was sponsored by Eileen Garrett's Parapsychology Foundation to work with researchers in the United States. His investigators include W. G. Roll of the Psychical Research Foundation, Durham, North Carolina, Dr. Thelma Moss of the University of California at Los Angeles, and Dr. Stanley Krippner of the Maimonides Dream Laboratory, Brooklyn.

Maintaining for many years an apartment in the seaside resort community of Brighton, Johnson has a new bachelor apartment in London's Chelsea section not far from the College of Psychic Science, where he works for most of the year.

The rest of the year is often spent in the United States and Canada lecturing and giving private sittings. As probably the most "experimented on" medium in the world today, Johnson even now cheerfully agrees to almost any experimental conditions in attempts to probe "the extentions of the mind."

PSYCHIC: How did your mediumship begin?
JOHNSON: I think I was always psychic. I am told that when I was about six years old—we lived in London and my grandmother lived miles away by the seaside—that I used to say to my mother, "Granny is coming to lunch today." My mother used to say, "Nonsense." But my grandmother would arrive.

So I suppose I was born with a psychic gift. But I didn't practice professionally as medium until 1947 when I was discharged from the Royal Air Force after the war. Before that, of course, I did a considerable amount of psychic work with friends and I had sittings myself with many of the most famous sensitives of the day.

PSYCHIC: Who, for example?
JOHNSON: When I was about sixteen years old I had a sitting with Eileen Garrett in London at the British College of Psychic Science. It was about four o'clock on a winter's afternoon and was getting dusk. I was asked to sit down and Mrs. Garrett went into trance. It was a very remarkable séance. My mother appeared to communicate extremely well—I was called by my pet name and there were many other extremely evidential facts given.

By the time the sitting ended the room was dark. When Mrs. Garrett came out of her trance state and turned around to switch on a light by her side, she suddenly looked at me very surprised and said, "You're much too young to waste your money on me. You should be spending it on beer and girls."

So I told her she was my birthday present from an aunt.

PSYCHIC: When was your first experience with trance?
JOHNSON: When I was about fifteen years old, and it was extremely alarming. I had been taken to some kind of development class by a lady I knew in England. It was in the summer and the room was small and rather stuffy.

Suddenly I felt as if I were going to faint. I knew that we weren't meant to break the circle [everyone was holding hands], and I thought this feeling would go off. The next thing I knew, I was given a glass of water by my host. I was very apologetic; I said I had never fainted before and I couldn't understand it. But he said, "Have a look at your watch." And to my astonishment it was three-quarters of an hour later. I was told I had gone into the trance state and someone had been speaking through me.

PSYCHIC: Who did they say had been speaking through you?

JOHNSON: The control that wanted to be known by the name of "Chiang." This frightened me very much, and I determined not to have anything to do with psychic things for an awful long time. I lived in fear it would come on at school or on a bus or something.

PSYCHIC: When did the personality Chiang come again?

JOHNSON: Well, after a while, my alarm subsided a bit as nothing more with trance seemed to happen. But there were some old friends of my parents who ran a home group, and during my school holidays I used to visit them once a week in the evening. It was with them that I developed my mediumship and I began to go into trance quite easily. Indeed, until twenty years ago I didn't know I could do psychic work unless I was in trance. I did all my work in trance then.

PSYCHIC: What did people say about the results they got from you?

JOHNSON: Fortunately, my results have always been pretty consistent. Of course, they vary, as with any sensitive, but from the very beginning in the trance state I was told I seemed to be able to produce a remarkable number of hits.

PSYCHIC: Did you think this was with the help of Chiang?

JOHNSON: I believe so. When I was about eighteen I did a certain amount of normal psychometry in waking state. But then I didn't seem to get any contact with anybody who might have been deceased. This was purely on material matters that I would get various extransensory facts.

PSYCHIC: Were most of your sitters interested in communication with discarnates?

JOHNSON: In those days, they were very much so. Now, of course,

I get many people with varying interests, including scientists who are interested academically. And some people regard me as a sort of astral realtor and a marriage bureau and a few other things.

A lot of people come, I think, with no spiritual purpose at all. I prefer, myself, to work with scientific people to explore the extensions of the mind, and second, with people who are interested in the possibility of survival.

PSYCHIC: Have you had any personal experiences that to you indicate survival?

JOHNSON: Oh, well, I haven't ever had the slightest doubt, because since I was very young I have on occasion seen discarnate people who appear to me as absolutely as solid as ordinary people here on earth.

PSYCHIC: What sort of material generally comes through in survival sittings?

JOHNSON: This varies very much, I think, on the ability of the discarnate communicator as well as on how I'm feeling and the state of mind of the sitter. If these three factors blend—the discarnate, the sitter, and the sensitive—then the communication can flow very naturally.

I mentally ask the discarnates if possible to give me some evidence that will help in their identification. Sometimes this comes better than others.

I think proof of survival—absolute proof of survival—is exceedingly difficult to get. Sometimes one is able to obtain something which the sitter does not know and has to be checked. This seems to me the most likely proof simply because it cannot easily be put down to telepathy.

PSYCHIC: What has been your most dramatic experience suggesting survival?

JOHNSON: A few years ago I was with a friend having a glass of sherry in a bar in London, when I casually noticed at the bar a West Indian gentleman and with him an elderly colored lady in native dress. I was a bit surprised because in London they nearly all wear European clothes, and so I remarked to my friend, "Isn't that strange—look at that woman in native dress."

He looked over at the bar and said, "I don't see her. I can see a West Indian in an ordinary suit and sports jacket. She must be one of your spooks. You'd better go down and talk to her."

When I went to the bar, however, I couldn't see this woman in native dress. So I asked the West Indian man to bring his drink and join us. He looked a bit surprised, but agreed. As soon as he sat down, this elderly colored lady appeared again. Her words seemed to drop into my mind: "This is my son. He is going to do something very foolish tonight. Stop him!"

Well, I thought, he'll think I'm certainly crazy; however, I've nothing to lose. So I said to him, "Your mother has just told me that you're going to do something very foolish tonight—and you're not to do it."

At this he went a shade paler and said, "It could not be my mother. She is dead." And again it was as if this voice came into my mind: "Tell him that I was blind from birth, and that I can see again in the spirit world." When I repeated this, he went even paler and tears began to come into his eyes, and he said, "This must be my mother—tell her I won't do it."

Later he confessed that he was going to be a lookout for a bank robbery that night. But because of the warning he had not gone. The others had all been caught. Finally, he decided to go back to the West Indies to start anew. Now this seems to me a direct intervention from the next world from the mother who loves her son and is anxious to protect him from harm.

PSYCHIC: How do psychic impressions come to you ordinarily?

JOHNSON: I try to dissociate my mind from my surroundings and make it rather like a still pond, so that I may pick up ripples of thought. Occasionally I get mental pictures in the center of my forehead which are small but perfectly vivid and clear. Sometimes they are in color, sometimes in black and white, rather as if I were looking through the wrong end of a pair of binoculars. Often these pictures are symbolic.

PSYCHIC: Are you aware of anything when you are working in trance?

JOHNSON: I very often can hear for a while at first the voice that is speaking through me although I can't stop speaking, and then I lapse into a deeper state of trance in which I hear nothing. Toward the end of the session, I seem gradually to come to, so I very often hear the end part.

PSYCHIC: Have you any idea how the control works?

JOHNSON: Chiang has given a number of trance lectures which have been taped, and he says he does not enter directly into my body but that around each of us there is a field of force something like a magnetic field, termed by some the "aura." Chiang says that he stands closely in this field of force and manipulates me rather like a puppet.

PSYCHIC: Has Chiang described who he is and why he came?

JOHNSON: Chiang says that he was born about seven hundred years ago in China during the Han dynasty. He was the son of a wealthy landowner and he says that I was his younger brother in that lifetime.

As a young boy of about thirteen years, he was sent to Tibet where he studied psychic matters and meditation, and therefore he was specially qualified to work with people here on earth because he has a very great knowledge of occult matters.

I don't pretend to be able to say that I can check his identity; I certainly can't. But I accept Chiang for the quality and value of his work.

PSYCHIC: What sort of help does Chiang try to bring to people?

JOHNSON: Well, he doesn't ever attempt "communication"—by that I mean bringing evidence of discarnate people's identity. He talks about personality trends about which he often makes helpful comments; he gives advice on potential psychic ability; and he answers any kind of philosophical question if it is within his scope.

PSYCHIC: Have any scientists listened to Chiang?

JOHNSON: Oh yes. Many indeed, and I've even had bishops come to talk to him.

But I don't think the scientists have come to any conclusions about Chiang. If you know anything about scientists, they always say, "Well, this is very interesting and I'll let you know the results in about ten years' time."

But they are certainly convinced that it is not my ordinary personality, although I do not think they are necessarily convinced this is a discarnate person. And perhaps many of them think that it is a secondary personality induced by auto-hypnosis.

PSYCHIC: And what do you think?

JOHNSON: Well, as I have seen him clairvoyantly and once saw him materialize solidly, I haven't the slightest doubt that Chiang is a separate entity. But I think a part of me is necessarily a part of the communication.

Chiang himself says that if you are pouring water into any kind of container, it takes the shape of that container and therefore if he is speaking through me then a part of what comes through must also be shaped by the shape of my mind.

PSYCHIC: You said you saw Chiang materialize?

JOHNSON: Yes. This was in South Africa in 1963 when I was doing a lecture tour there. The famous Welsh materialization medium Alex Harris, who has now retired, was then living in South Africa. He invited me as a guest to their private group, and it was a very remarkable experience. A number of entities materialized and appeared to be as flesh and blood. Indeed Chiang materialized and to us he was absolutely solid. I held out my hand and he put one small hand with long fingernails on the top of my hand and a small hand underneath it and patted the top of my hand.

I was a bit overcome and said, "I don't know why you bother with me. I'm not a very good person." And he said, "We are not concerned with things of the earth in our world. We are concerned with honesty of purpose and kindness of heart." It was a most comforting remark.

PSYCHIC: Why do you think guides are so often exotic Eastern types?

JOHNSON: Well, the skeptic would say that they are more dramatic. But it may be that North American Indians, the ancient Egyptians, the Chinese, and so on, were brought up with a belief in communication with the next world. And therefore, when they go to the next world, they would have knowledge that would make it easier for them to control the necessary forces for communication. But I have to say that I do not know. I do know people who have European guides.

Too, I think guides are often a higher aspect of someone. They often appear to have a greater sense of wisdom and understanding than the person they come through. Therefore they are helpful, and I think one should accept them as that, though not as all-knowledgeable.

PSYCHIC: Have you found that all trance mediums have guides?

JOHNSON: I believe that not only all trance mediums have guides, I believe that all people have somebody from the other world who tries to help then along the path of life. They may not be conscious of them, and I'm quite certain that many guides must give up in absolute disgust, and say, "Well, I really can't do anything with this person—I'd better try somebody else."

PSYCHIC: Do you consider yourself a Spiritualist?

JOHNSON: In the beginning of my mediumship, I thought that everything I received psychically came from the next world. I was a Spiritualist then in outlook. Unless people had a purpose of communication with the next world, I wouldn't see them at all.

But now I believe that there are two separate forms of psychic ability—one in which you use your own psychic ability along a certain level; and another which is a kind of bridge between two worlds. It is like two levels of consciousness. One, the survival level, seems to hit me sideways from my right-hand side; and the extrasensory level, about material problems, seems to be on a parallel line to my sitter. It feels different.

I very often ask sitters if they are particularly interested in survival. Whereas, if they have a material or emotional problem, I wouldn't bother the next world with it. I can deal with it myself. When I am in touch with a discarnate, I get rather an excited electrical feeling which is quite different from ordinary ESP.

PSYCHIC: Why have you chosen to become a medium?

JOHNSON: On occasion people come to me in great distress, not necessarily through bereavement, but maybe they are in some great trouble that could be material or psychological. And often it is possible to be of some little assistance to them. That is certainly one of the reasons.

Second, I am interested in anything to do with the study of extensions of the mind. I think this is why I have been experimented on by scientists very extensively, and I have never objected to any kind of experiment. I believe that we are in the horse stage compared to the jet age in knowledge of the latent parts of the mind.

PSYCHIC: What are some of the experiments that you've undertaken with scientists?

JOHNSON: Oh, I've done haunted houses and I have worked in scientists' laboratories with thirteen electrodes stuck on my head going to an EEG machine while I have psychometrized objects in sealed envelopes. I have done this in the waking state, in deep hypnosis, and in the self-induced trance state.

PSYCHIC: How about the investigation of haunted houses?

JOHNSON: This always sounds enormously exciting and romantic. Whereas many of them I think are of psychometric origin, that is, not a real ghost. Some event has taken place that is impregnated within the framework of the house and sensitive people are able to pick up the feeling of horror or fright and even events, just as I can pick up things by holding somebody's wristwatch. There have been occasions in which I think there has been genuine haunting.

PSYCHIC: Do you ever get communication or impressions from the living?

JOHNSON: Oh, yes. One can by mistake think one is in touch with the discarnate and find one is talking with the living.

I had an experience like this when a lady came to see me, and I correctly said that she had been living in Australia with an elderly male relative. I said that he had passed on and was here. I described quite accurately that he had a beard and that he had lost a leg. She said, "Oh, yes, that must be my old uncle. The poor man was very sick, and I'm very glad to know he's gone. And I'm absolutely delighted from an evidential point of view because my sister is still with him, and she's never believed in psychic things, and so this will be good evidence to convince her."

Well, the surprising, and to me, somewhat disappointing result was that when she telephoned her sister in Australia, she found that the old man had not died. Because of the difference in time, though, he had been asleep, and it may be that his astral or etheric body had been traveling at this time, and it was that which I picked up at this séance. I'm told that he died about two months later.

PSYCHIC: Do you encourage people to develop their psychic ability?

JOHNSON: If I think they've got anything worth developing, yes. Many people seem to think that everybody's psychic. I personally don't believe that any more than that everybody is musical. I think it's just a gift that comes to some. There's a difference between sensitivity and true psychic ability.

A lot of people are sensitive and may be intuitive, but if anybody has true psychic ability, then it's rather like discovering somebody with musical ability who in the end will become an opera singer, and there are very few.

PSYCHIC: How about spirituality? Do you think that is necessary?

JOHNSON: I think it is also important, yes. But I think psychic gifts come to all sorts of people. For example, surely you can have one singer who leads an extremely spiritual life, but you can have another singer who leads a life which is the very reverse and may have an even better voice.

However, I think spirituality is helpful, because surely this should help with integrity. I think integrity is of enormous importance, and if people haven't got this, then they should leave psychic things alone.

PSYCHIC: What sort of methods do you teach for psychic development?

JOHNSON: I teach meditation. And I think it is very important when people are beginning to receive psychic impressions to endeavor to sort out that which is possibly imagination and association of ideas from the true content of the psychic impression.

PSYCHIC: And how can they learn to do this?

JOHNSON: Practice, practice, practice, and patience. Horrible words beginning with a "p" which nobody likes.

PSYCHIC: Do you encourage people to train to become mediums?

JOHNSON: If they've got anything, yes. I think that perhaps people are inclined to leap into something a bit too quickly and get too enthusiastic at the beginning and think that everything is going to happen at once when usually it is a long slow process involving a great deal of discipline and hard work, which most people aren't prepared to put into it.

I think that in the old days, when I was younger, there were certainly less distractions, such as television. Therefore, people were more prepared to devote a whole evening once a week, regularly. Now there are so many distractions people don't want to give up anything.

PSYCHIC: What does Chiang think about developing mediumship?

JOHNSON: Chiang has said that psychic phenomena are not important in themselves unless they arouse within people the knowledge that there is something beyond this world. To develop psychically just to be able to astonish your friends is not a purpose at all.

Chiang used to ask prospective students, "What is your purpose? Look into your heart and if you believe you may be of more service to humanity, then develop. But if you can only say it might be rather interesting, then it's not worth doing."

PSYCHIC: How do you feel about the so-called Age of Aquarius?

JOHNSON: Chiang has quite an interesting remark to make about this. He says that the birth of a new age takes place around every two thousand years, and the last age was the Piscean Age.

But the birth of anything is painful. A woman in the early months of gestation is very uncomfortable some of the time, and as in little things, so in big things.

So there is bound to be disturbance at the beginning of a new age; there's bound to be disruption; there's bound to be racial disagreement. It's rather like boiling a pot of soup; all the scum comes to the surface, and then if you skim this off, there is the pure soup underneath.

PSYCHIC: And how do you think this "pure soup" will turn out?

JOHNSON: I think that the tremendously encouraging thing about this new age is quite definitely the young people. When I lectured years ago to audiences—and I've done this many years—perhaps the average age of the audience was forty-five upward. Now I find about half my audiences are twenty-five downward. I think this is enormously encouraging and I find the young much more intelligent in inquiring than when I was young.

And although there are so many difficulties and distractions, fundamentally, I think they have a great wish and desire to find something to hold on to and to find a truth that may help in this life.

PSYCHIC: What is your philosophy of life?

JOHNSON: This is, of course, personal—I believe that all religions are the same and that the central theme in all faiths is surely brotherhood.

I think that religions—orthodox religions—are helpful to many people. They are like staircases, but with differently shaped handrails. It doesn't matter which rail you take hold of as long as it's helpful to you at the time, and therefore, I think the earth is an evolutionary process—and my religion is to try to live a life of brotherhood.

PSYCHIC: Do you believe in reincarnation?

JOHNSON: I have no proof of this, but it seems to me entirely logical. Some inner part of me believes in it implicitly, and I do believe in it without any proof.

PSYCHIC: How do you think reincarnation fits into the purpose of life?

JOHNSON: Chiang says that the purpose of life is evolution in a spiritual way—the gradual overcoming through a process of living on earth many times, the earthly temptations which assail us here. Too strong appetites, perhaps, in certain directions—envy, jealousy of our fellow man.

When eventually the soul force that is incarnate on this earth has overcome all these things, so that its love is a true love and an impersonal love that only wishes well for its fellow man, so that he loves his neighbor or the man who is disfigured in the street, then it is probably no longer necessary to come back to the earth plane. It is the sins of the mind and the spirit, not physical things, which have to be overcome.

When you have overcome these things, it is no longer necessary to incarnate again on earth. Then you go through a process which Chiang terms "second death"—a death of the spiritual in which you go on to a much higher sphere where you are a teacher and an initiate.

PSYCHIC: Then what is your concept of God?

JOHNSON: I suppose this question has been asked millions of times to millions of different people. Chiang speaks of the hierarchy of good that is termed "God." And all I can tell you is that I believe there is a power or some powers of good which we can term "God."

[Following are excerpts from trance sittings with Douglas Johnson in which Chiang answers some questions.]

PSYCHIC: Chiang, could you describe your world?

CHIANG: In our world everyone perceives each other as solid as you do on earth. However, our bodies vibrate at a faster rate than yours, and therefore we are invisible to you.

Our world resembles yours in having different states of consciousness and understanding. Those who are interested in things of the mind tend to be with others of the same outlook; those who are interested only in material things tend to mix with others of like taste.

In our dimension, however, there are many activities that have no parallel at all. There are whole ranges of color that are not existent in your spectrum. We also have things that you have, such as music and all the arts. The range of interest is vast.

Because we are in another dimension, many people think that we are all-seeing and all-knowing. But that is not true. I have been asked to explain nuclear physics, of which I know nothing, nor could I explain anything about your earthly stocks and shares, and if I could, I would not. No, there is work to do in other directions. As I am a helper with this instrument, so each of you has a helper in our world who seeks to light a little path that is so often fraught with difficulties.

It is part of our work to give an inner sense of stability; a balance between the practical and impractical, blended so that there is a

wider path toward understanding an inner happiness and peace.
PSYCHIC: What is your philosophy of life?
CHIANG: The soul force, when it is incarnated, brings with it, without conscious memory, experiences of earlier lives. Because they lack this memory, people may sometimes complain, "Why should this happen to me?" Yet there is a perfect balance and a perfect justice —the scales of each one's life are balanced.

If you were in the position of seeing the complete series of your lives, you would quickly understand the reason for apparent difficulties and unfairness. In the same way you can earn difficulties in the present life. If there is grave failure in your present life, then there must be a repetition in the next life. Since the next life should be one of expansion and not of repetition, it is a waste of time.

Even in the present life, you can look back on certain failings and find that there is a pattern of repetition—the same mistake over and over. Then it is time to alter it, so that you don't have to repeat the same mistake in future lives.

Remember, if things seem to you unfair, realize that although you have not consciously attracted this to you, it is there for a purpose, possibly something you were not able to overcome in an earlier life.

If you have been born to many burdens, then you have been born with the inner strength to overcome them. If you accept that which seems inevitable with an inner strength and determination to overcome with understanding, you will build an integrated and expanded personality.

You have had many lives. You have many to come. Do not worry if you fail many times, for all fail many times. There is always another opportunity. The process of many worlds and many lives is evolutionary, and its purpose is to gain understanding.

May your footsteps walk in peace.

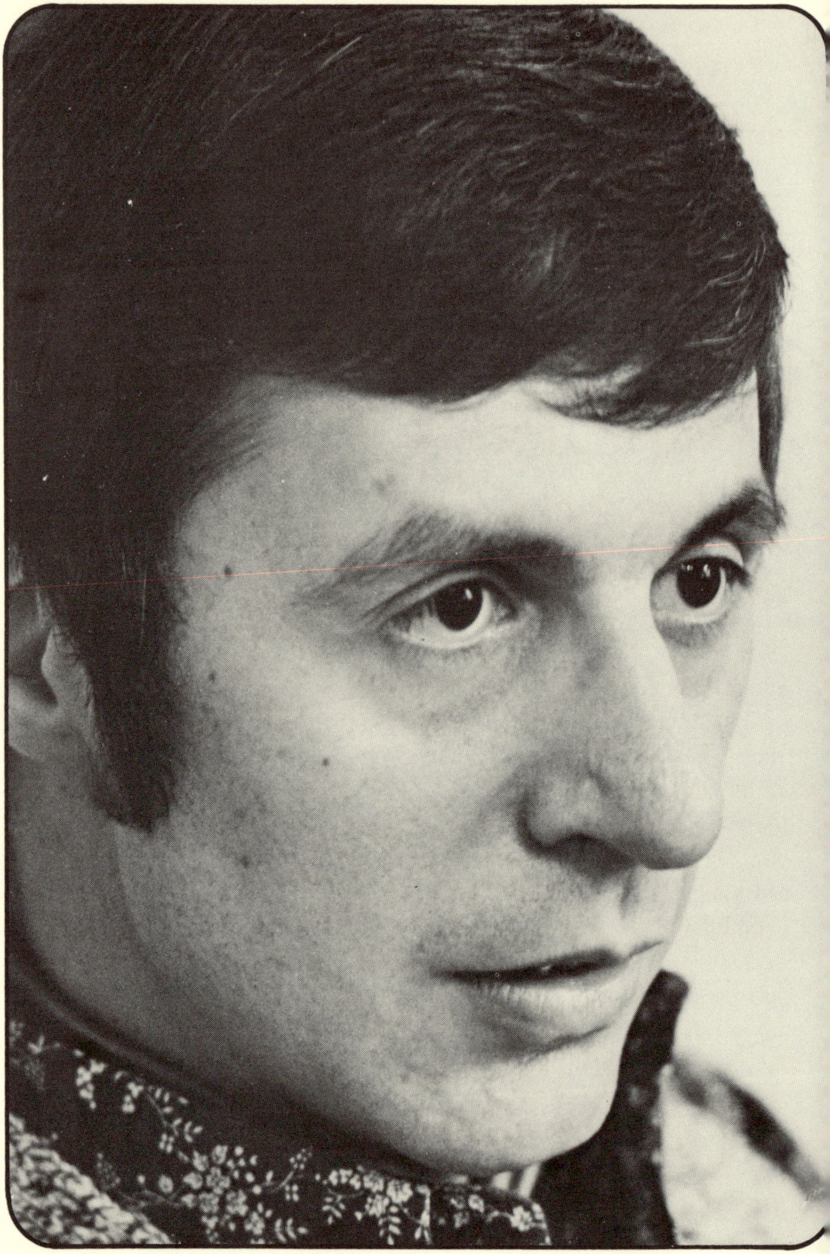

seven
Kreskin

Kreskin, often billed "The Amazing Kreskin," was born George Kresge in the mid-1930s in West Caldwell, New Jersey, where he grew up and attended school. His mother and father, Mr. and Mrs. George Kresge, still make the family home there.

Beginning his career unusually early, Kreskin was performing half-hour shows around the country as a traveling magician when he was nine, and at eleven was using hypnosis in his programs. According to the New York Times, he was probably the youngest performing hypnotist in the world, but about those early hypnotic presentations he says, "I think more people fell asleep in the audience than on the stage."

His serious interest in the field began at five and by the time he was ten, he had read the entire psychology department of the adult branch of his hometown library. Today, he has built up his own personal reference library to almost 3,000 volumes on various subjects ranging from fundamental magic and hypnosis to telepathy and parapsychology.

One of the most powerful influences in Kreskin's decision to become a mentalist-magician was the once popular comic strip "Mandrake the Magician." It was "Mandrake," he says, that prompted him at the age of five to pursue the art and learn card and other traditional magician tricks. It was also "Mandrake" who stimulated his interest in ESP.

As early as eight he began "fooling around" with ESP, when he thought it would be a good trick to be able to pick up the thoughts, instead of spoken words, of his playmates in the game "Hot and Cold." (In the game, an object is hidden from one of the players and the others direct him to it by saying "hot" or "cold.") Kreskin practiced on his younger brother for over three months before getting what he considered were encouraging results.

It was from this childhood game that his "check test" feat emerged, in which he invites anyone to hide the fee for his performance, and if he can't find it through ESP, he forfeits payment. He claims he has forfeited a fee on only one occasion, when he was suffering from an eye injury and could not concentrate.

After completing high school in Caldwell, New Jersey, he entered Seton Hall University in South Orange, where he earned an A.B. degree in psychology. It was during college that he took the name Kreskin, which he compiled from parts of his own name and from the names of two traditional magicians he most respected. From Harry Kellar, one of America's first great magicians, he took "K," and from Houdin, a Frenchman and one of the world's great conjurers, he took "in." Kreskin is now his stage as well as legal name.

As a popular mentalist, Kreskin has performed across the country in night clubs, colleges, and special concerts, in addition to presenting business seminars and once practicing as a professional hypnotist in the psychology community. Recently, over the past several years, he has begun to appear more frequently on national television with personalities such as Mike Douglas, Johnny Carson, Steve Allen, Dinah Shore, Merv Griffin, and Phyllis Diller. Today he is booked six to eight months in advance.

An energetic and hyperactive individual (he reads 7,000 words a minute), Kreskin is now airing his own TV show ("The Amazing World of Kreskin") in the United States and Canada, acting a part in a new mystery movie in which he plays himself, and, officially, publicly representing Big Brothers of America, an organization of which he is a member and which promotes companionship for young, fatherless boys.

In addition, he devised a popular game called "Kreskin's ESP," which has sold millions of sets. Marketed by the Milton Bradley Company, it is now being distributed worldwide. As a serious offshoot of his game, Kreskin has introduced a system for conditioning the mind for concentration and meditation. Marketed by the 3M Company, it is called "Kreskin's Krystal."

About his talents, Psychology Professor Frank Murphy of Seton Hall has theorized that "Kreskin has developed a strikingly unique and different method of communication, which may take more than fifty years to become common." Mike Douglas has said he is "unique and utterly baffling," while comedienne Phyllis Diller mused, "He is a male witch and ought to be burned at the stake."

Riding the crest of today's intense interest in things psychic and explorations of the mind, Kreskin has come of his own after nearly thirty years of developing his mentalist-hypnotist performance and "influencing other people's thoughts with his own."

PSYCHIC: Are you psychic?
KRESKIN: If you're asking if I manifest phenomena that fit in the category of being psychic, I would say, yes, under certain conditions. But I would prefer to say that what I do is hypersensitive or hypernormal, rather than extrasensitive.

I think a great deal of phenomena that happens in the field of parapsychology is related to the senses in terms we've never been able to compartmentalize. We have blurred it by saying it's ESP.

If a person thinks about it, ESP is an abortive contradiction. It suggests that we have an ability to perceive beyond our senses. How can we have a sense beyond our senses? Maybe we should just expand the five senses to six or seven or even twenty-two.

So in this light, I would say that I do manifest some of what we call ESP. But I don't do it under just *any* conditions; I have to control my conditions.

PSYCHIC: Controlling conditions to make people think that something paranormal is occurring or really making it occur?

KRESKIN: Both, it depends on the circumstances. For example, what I do in my concerts—as I like to call them—is create an extremely sensitive rapport with my audience, whereby my subjects are as much in tune with me as I am with them. The equipment in my presentations, despite myself, is something outside of me—the personalities of people around me.

It isn't just my mood, either. Sure, I take my one-mile walk before every television show or concert to detach myself from the distracting things around me and to build up an attitude of deep introspection. I also bring myself to a point where it doesn't for one moment enter my mind that anything can go wrong to destroy what I'm achieving in my presentation. I go in so positive that I believe no matter what happens I can harness some reaction from the people I'm working with—I never think of the negative factors. Perhaps in terms of your readers what I do is "psych" myself up.

PSYCHIC: This sounds like some form of suggestion or subtly getting people to do or to believe what you are.

KRESKIN: That's a factor, sure. For years I was known as a mentalist and a hypnotist, but I have since come to the conclusion that hypnosis, perhaps as you and I and everyone thinks of it, really doesn't exist.

I think one of the functional myopias in this society is that we have overlooked the power of suggestion. And it's sad we've been left behind in this area by the Eastern part of the world—India, Asia, and now the Russians.

For instance, in a séance where genuine manifestations may take place, there's also the factor that educated, intelligent, trained people can be hallucinating and seeing things that are not there. Just place someone in total darkness for a sustained period of time where you have the interaction of other people and his imagination can play dramatic influences on his perceptions. Keep in mind, too, that there's also greater sensitivity, emotion, and expectation in this kind of a setting.

So my program is an excursion for me and my audience—partly through suggestion—into some of the real dramatic aspects of our life, which most of us encounter every day.

PSYCHIC: Then you're saying that you are not a psychic?

KRESKIN: That's right. I am not a psychic. I don't give readings and I don't predict the future. But I have produced manifestations that perhaps are attached to the psychic side—or the hypersensitive side as I call it—a lot of which I don't yet understand. Obviously, something does happen and suddenly I'm talking about things I shouldn't be able to know, and I don't even understand why they're coming to me.

So I don't feel it's necessary to say that a particular thing is psychic, because it's just as easy to call what's happening a subconscious-level response manifested through hypersensitivity. Perhaps I've just conditioned myself to create this more easily.

PSYCHIC: Perhaps you should be billed as a hypnotist.

KRESKIN: Well, I've practiced hypnosis professionally for many years and once had an office with Dr. Harold Hansen, a New Jersey psychologist. But hypnosis is just part of it, and no longer in the formal sense.

One of the burning ambitions of my life is to contribute to this field by showing the world that hypnosis, the hypnotic trance, is nonexistent. But I don't mean to say that people are faking it.

What is unknown to most physicians and professional people, as well as lay hypnotists, is that if you give a person who is hypnotized, supposedly in a deep trance, a lie detector test (polygraph) you find that the subject knows everything that is going on. He is perfectly aware of the true state of affairs.

For example, I will set up a demonstration with any physician anywhere using a polygraph to prove that a subject, with whom we produce complete hypnotic analgesia, really knowns every moment that a pin pricks the hand. It's only that his mind has distorted pain as pressure.

Also, we can take the same subject and record his brain-wave patterns on an electroencephalograph machine to prove the point. In a person deeply unconscious these patterns change, but we find that the person in "deep trance" produces brain-wave patterns as if he were totally awake—so in truth he must be.

And *anything* that has ever been done with a person in so-called deep hypnosis can be displayed without going to the trouble of hypnotizing him if two things are done: one, he gives you his attention and trust; and two, the suggestions are administered in a skillful way.

This is something the psychics and the people who examine séances, as well as those who examine dramatic response in the laboratory, must start to become aware of.

PSYCHIC: How do you describe yourself, then?

KRESKIN: I suppose as a hypersensitist, a mentalist, and also a mental wizard. People have asked me why I don't call myself a sensitive or some kind of psychic name rather than a mentalist. There's a reason. I decided very early in my life that I have to be brutally honest about my work because I believe in it, and because I have such a bad memory that if I had to cover up I'd be in a real mess.

As for my own ability to pick up information through telepathy or however—and people could say it's a kind of muscle reading or cues given unconsciously that I perceive which very well may be a factor —Dr. Harold Hansen and a number of others with whom I've worked, have said: "It's perhaps better you don't know everything that's happening when you're presenting your program, because obviously at some point in your show you're harnessing something more than you'd be able to if you were self-conscious of what's happening."

In the classic literature during the early period of the British Society for Psychical Research a word used to describe thought perception was "hyperaesthesia," whereby an individual becomes sensitive to the slightest details and the slightest changes in smell and other sense functions. Perhaps I utilize this, on a subconscious level, without being aware of it.

Also, I have developed to a point in my work whereby I can apply suggestion nonverbally; perhaps even here some telepathic force enters in. So it is not unusual in my program for me to have someone respond to a suggestion I did not verbally give. People will no doubt ask, "Did the subject somehow sense by my motions the response desired?" I don't think so.

But I have to qualify this by saying that I cannot totally control the ESP factor. Fortunately, I have enough of a foundation with what ability I may have in creating suggestible responses, utilizing my magician's repertoire, and so on, that I can build on this foundation and play by ear until I create the proper tone. It may take ten to fifteen minutes, but my audience isn't aware that my program is changing format, because everything is part of it.

As for the term "mentalist," I use it because of what I do and because of the free license I have as an entertainer to extend myself and my program.

PSYCHIC: Do you feel bound by an entertainer's or a magician's code not to reveal the tricks of your act?

KRESKIN: Yes, because when I think of the years of training I have gone through and of the strong discipline I have endured—practicing seven or more hours a day—to reach this point in my career, then I think it's unfair to the tradition of the magician. Furthermore, formal magic plays only a small part in my work.

I also think it would be unfair to my audience, except that they must realize that playing cards are notoriously manipulative.

On the other hand, traditional magicians are supposed to be totally, unalterably skeptical of any manifestation of psi phenomena.

And knowing some magicians, I'm always impressed that these men can be authorities on their own point of view. Yet men can believe anything so clearly and so strongly that despite evidence or proof, they will not change their convictions. A good example of this was the scientists who witnessed first hand Alexander Graham Bell demonstrate the telephone and who concluded: "That's ventriloquism." And I suppose they were correct to their own viewpoint.

So it's interesting that Houdini, one of the greatest magicians of our century, successfully exposed many mediums. There was probably a need for it then, as now, since there has always been abuse in the field. But I honestly believe that this great man would have exposed the most legitimate medium as a fraud, because one sees things as one expects to see them. In psychology this is called apperception.

So when we look at this part of Houdini's life and that of most of his colleagues, we realize that when they said there was nothing to psychic phenomena, nothing to ESP, in their naïveté they were being rather myopic and narrow-minded.

PSYCHIC: You believe there are genuine psychics, mediums?
KRESKIN: Yes, I believe there are people who are sensitive and who can display ESP.

But I want to bring out my criticism of some of these so-called magicians who feel that they have to prove that something is totally fraudulent. They are as blind as the person who accepts all psychic phenomena purely on statement.

PSYCHIC: What ingredients do you use in your concerts?
KRESKIN: Conjuring, thought perception, telepathic phenomena, subconscious sensitivity, suggestibility, and humor, which I also need because not only must I inject this for my audience, but for myself, too, to break the binding tension I'm under. You see, I have a very high metabolic rate, I eat five meals a day and I sometimes lose two pounds a show.

But anyone who has seen my concerts probably knows there are three basic aspects to them: magic, thought reading, and suggestion. In approximate percentages, conjuring—in the traditional sense of magic—might be ten to fifteen percent, while classic, clear-cut suggestibility is perhaps fifty percent of the presentation. The remainder is ESP. But ESP often varies with the concert and the audience.

If I'm having difficulty establishing a rapport with my audience, the ESP portion could be only twenty percent, but it can climb to sixty-five percent when the audience and I are in tune—I can roll on and on. Also, I discovered that I had to condition my audience, which is really the secret of what I do.

PSYCHIC: What are some of your classical tricks and how do you do them?

KRESKIN: In these cases, I don't use the word "trick" but, rather, "effect," because of the mental effort involved. One I like to do is have someone pick a telephone directory at random from a large pile of directories, open it to any page, and then put his finger on a specific name—a name which I have written out before the test.

How is this done? I can't explain it fully, but what I do is create such a rapid, intensive rapport with the subject that I cause him to respond to my thoughts, directing him somehow to the correct directory, the correct page, and then the word or name I want—sort of telepathy in reverse.

This last part is done by asking the subject to rotate his arm about the page, tightening the circle with each rotation. While he's doing this and my back is to him, I mentally visualize the circle and where the hand will stop—or should stop. Somehow by mental imagery, by suggestion, he picks up nonverbally what I desire—he's feeling and doing it.

PSYCHIC: What about the watch effect?

KRESKIN: Well, in this I get a person to rotate the hands of somebody else's watch and stop them to match my watch, which is later given to someone not participating in the test to hold and check. I do not see the person spin the stem since my back is turned. But I am also spinning the stem of my watch to synchronize with where I think he'll stop—where I want him to stop.

In this case it is a sympathetic reaction between two people; I'm controlling the response, but I cannot always do it. In fact, one of the negative highlights of my career is that it failed recently.

PSYCHIC: I suppose anyone can say you prearranged this with your subjects.

KRESKIN: Absolutely not! That's why I have an offer of twenty thousand dollars to anyone who can prove I use confederates. I don't. Besides, I find I function better not meeting people before the show; it's more legitimate and more dramatic.

PSYCHIC: How do you receive information when it comes through mental impressions—symbols, images, sounds?

KRESKIN: I don't receive things in symbols, but I do practice automatic writing—I've practiced it for years. And I don't consider it psychic.

When I'm talking to an audience, I'm usually constantly writing. And it's almost as if my hand is unconsciously writing material—way ahead of what I'm saying to my audience. I'm constantly working ahead. So that's one way I express my information.

The other way is in some form of visual or auditory imagery, in which I almost see a picture or hear information—which I don't really hear. It could be called clairaudience, except I think it's just my way of handling the information, of being hypersensitive.

I've even been asked if I have an outside "control" or spirit guide. I have to say no, I don't think so, since I believe it's my imagination that does this.

PSYCHIC: How do the images appear to you?

KRESKIN: They appear to me commonly with my eyes open as I'm looking over the audience. In the case of reading a social security number, I see it in a sequence more easily over a darkened part of the theater, which acts like a blackboard for me. I don't see with my mind, but I can project the number with my eyes open, visualize the numbers instantly. And at the same time I start to speak, I start to write.

The great problem here, though, is my reasoning factor, which has always been my worst enemy. Because if I start to evaluate critically, I destroy whatever I'm getting naturally. It has to come impulsively, spontaneously, which in itself is the kind of training you have to learn to harness.

PSYCHIC: Did you develop or discover your ability to do this?

KRESKIN: I think both. But I also think a person has to have inherently a potential in the field. The turning point in my life was when I learned there was more to communicating with a person than talking, listening, looking, touching—or tasting and smelling food.

But keep in mind I have spent years studying and perfecting what I do today. For example, I am capable of deep concentration, which enables me to produce partly what I do. In a matter of minutes I can produce most of the manifestations we would describe as hypnotic. I can lower my pulse rate in a matter of a couple of minutes—down to fifteen to eighteen beats a minute. [Normal average pulse rate is 72.] I do this by thinking of the most tranquil, calm imagery for myself I can.

By holding that imagery, and for myself adding a total bluelike quality to it in a setting of trees, I'm able to create this tremendous relaxation of my metabolic rate. If I change it to red and bring running horses into the imagery, my pulse rate rises. So I don't say, "My pulse is going down, I'm relaxing"—that's verbal rhetoric, without the quality of an emotional tie.

PSYCHIC: Have you been tested in any parapsychological laboratories?

KRESKIN: Not in a formal one, no. But I've been tested at Seton Hall University in an informal way by Professor Murphy of the Psychology Department there. He has stated that what I have developed is a strikingly unique and different method of communication, which may take fifty years or more to become common.

Also, Dr. Harold Hansen once said that if he could somehow pinpoint my methods and techniques—not just the concentration but the outer manifestations as well—this might be of use in psychology and psychotherapy.

PSYCHIC: Why haven't you submitted to formal testing?

KRESKIN: I suppose everyone has a rationalization, a cop-out. For me I'm sure I wouldn't function anywhere near my capacity in a laboratory setting because I can't stress highly enough. I function best in my own world, with the emotional stimuli. I have to do what I do, to do my thing.

In this context, too, I think we have to look at the history of laboratory experimentation in this field, which seems to show that "the thing" that's trying to be captured or studied diminishes appreciably.

Dr. Soal, a notable psychical researcher of England, often mentioned this, saying that even the best sensitives' abilities gradually diminished in the cold, laboratory setting.

I think scientists are going to have to meet sensitive people halfway; they're going to have to spend time testing a subject in his own environment, his own world, and not always just theirs.

But it would give me much pleasure to have some psychologists follow me and study me in my own setting to see what can be gathered. It would be difficult on my schedule, though.

PSYCHIC: It sounds as though you have some definite opinions about parapsychology.

KRESKIN: I think Dr. Rhine and his work were twenty years ahead of his time and made a great contribution. Today, however, I think they are twenty years behind the time.

Parapsychologists haven't changed in their experimentation, though they have better machines for measuring now.

But in my observation, the study of ESP has gone through two stages: the collection of spontaneous phenomena, and the experimental laboratory stage, which has bogged the field down in America. Science shouldn't have to stay in the laboratory, because the emotional factor—a key ingredient in this whole field—is so often left out of the laboratory and you cannot easily create emotions there. Some of the profound data, such as deathlike images and accident-like situations, involve emotional ties. So I think we must keep the emotional factor as part of the research and seek it in its natural setting, wherever that may be.

PSYCHIC: Some parapsychologists are concerned over the popularity and commercialization of the field, which they think are detrimental to its progress. Obviously you don't agree.

KRESKIN: I do in part, since I think a lot of the popular, written material which is presented as fact should be presented for what it is—speculation. I also think the field's popularity is going to continue to increase due to the great stress and uncertainty in the world today, despite concern of some parapsychologists, because the popular interest this time is different. We don't have a vast lunatic fringe; rather, we have a tremendous amount of writers, scientists, and sophisticated people from every walk of life with a very serious interest, which I'm convinced is here to stay.

Scientists shouldn't forget that the popularity and commercialization of a subject in any culture is reflective of the interest of the culture at that time. So one wouldn't be there if the other weren't.

We all need the public for support and for developing these fields, because when they are isolated in the laboratory in the hands of the self-appointed, privileged few, then they usually become lost or set aside for something else—or are never fully accepted.

This happened with the traditional medical hypnotist, who said, "... only in the laboratory, only in the medical office." Yet through the years when no one paid attention to hypnosis or the laboratory experimenters, it took the lowly stage hypnotist to manifest the public's interest enough finally to bring it to the serious attention of today's medical fraternity, despite over two centuries of being around. It was finally accepted in the early history of medicine—as early as 1958! That's progress?

PSYCHIC: What makes you think the ESP field will remain a popular one?

KRESKIN: I think people are discovering and realizing that despite the tremendous advancement in science, technology, and the greater comfort of living, man's problems are more, not less. Consequently, there is a greater searching, and when man searches he's likely to turn toward a more inward or spiritual plane and a less physical one, even though ESP may in essence be physical.

And so the question and the reasoning about man has come down to the level of the young people, who are idealists. Perhaps in their search they are also seeking to get away from this plane, whether it be through meditation, through introspection, the Eastern philosophies, drugs, or whatever.

PSYCHIC: Is this why you travel and perform the college circuit?

KRESKIN: Yes. Most young people are deeply involved in at least one aspect of this field with an open-minded, analytical interest. I think that's healthy.

At the opposite end of the scale, though, is the drug problem, which I think is very unhealthy and which I am convinced is one of the greatest potentials for destroying our society.

The one hope that I can see is that the college students interested in this field will, as time goes by, become realistic about the limitations and dangers of drugs, while at the same time they will become aware of the potentials of the psychic field—that they can seek inward awareness through meditation, through a mental approach without a chemical.

PSYCHIC: What is your philosophy of life?

KRESKIN: First I should say that I believe in God very deeply. But I don't claim to know God.

One of my deepest philosophies is that we are responsible for what we do. I think we answer to someone when we go—even if it's to ourselves.

I think the philosophy of reincarnation which is becoming so popular—and which I don't believe in—has supplied a cop-out for many. They think somehow they'll come back to a better life, or if they fail this one they can do it over.

So in the end, whether I'm successful, whatever I achieve in my life, whatever I create, is because I did it. If it's wrong, then I am responsible and somehow reparation will have to be made.

Personally, I believe in the hereafter, my religion is predicated on it; yet what I am saying is that we can't prove it. And it's an annoying dilemma and enigma for those people who believe in Spiritualism and who can't set up an experiment for absolute proof, because every piece of information can always be explained by telepathy.

PSYCHIC: Then apparently what you do doesn't conflict with your philosophy and religious outlook.

KRESKIN: I think it would if I used what I do to influence others negatively, in the sense of taking away from them—depriving them of religious concepts, defrauding them, misrepresenting myself—but I don't. I'm no more or less than I claim to be.

I'm Roman Catholic and I have a minor degree in Catholic philosophy. I should say that in the beginning it seemed to be in conflict because of the theories and misunderstandings and superstitions about this field, but it isn't. Perhaps the people will ask whether I am implying that the miracles recorded in the Bible are purely psychic phenomena. Well, I haven't caused the water to separate through suggestion or concentration.

But I do think that some hypnotic-like phenomena entered into some of these manifestations because I believe our Maker placed in us many potentials which He made natural. Perhaps the sin is that, as the years have gone by, we have lost use of the techniques to make use of these potentials and natural abilities.

PSYCHIC: In your own philosophy, then, what do you think man's role in the universe is?

KRESKIN: My feeling philosophically and religiously is that man is not fated. I don't believe that his life is predestined. I am convinced that man possesses a free will, which is why he is responsible.

I believe strongly that he was placed on earth for a reason which shows itself in the talent he exhibits—and that goes for all talents. It is the message he brings to life and the continued growth of knowledge he contributes.

So I feel each person on earth in some way is here to contribute to the inevitable higher development of society. But the problem is that with the freedom of will and man's freedom to choose, this potential is often abused or used to destroy. Consequently, we have leaders with tremendous capacities to lead, who are the natural hypnotists.

And I don't think there will ever be a heaven on earth. Somehow I think that our Maker has made that on another plane, because it seems man doesn't create as well or work as hard when he has things totally pleasurable.

PSYCHIC: What do you intend to accomplish with your career and by what you do?

KRESKIN: I have three things in life that I would like very much: I'd like the luxury and the responsibility of true friends; I'd like the satisfaction and the tremendous work and development necessary in producing a family; and finally I'd like the satisfaction of knowing that I caused millions of people around the world to realize that there are more things than we've been told exist. Perhaps any feeling of philosophy and wonderment I stimulate will cause them to think more seriously about life and begin searching for its true essence and meaning.

But above all I hope never to be considered an exposer of psychic phenomena or never a blind accepter of all that has taken place, either. I'd like to be considered an entertaining pioneer or a pioneer in entertainment, that's all.

I can realize my greatest potential as an entertainer who uses suggestion and ESP. This is my niche and I feel that it gives me an opportunity to communicate certain truths in a very dramatic way.

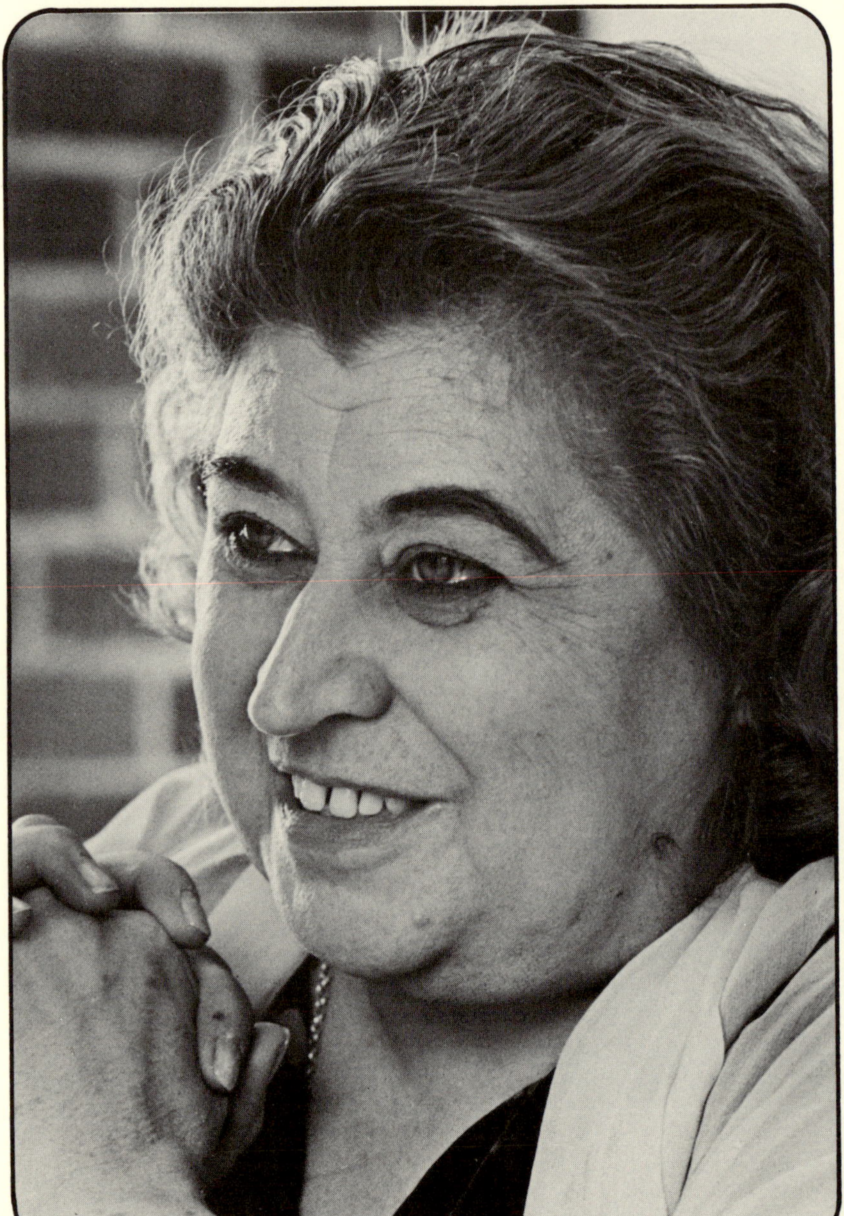

eight
Sybil Leek

Sybil Leek traces her witch's heritage to A.D. 1134 on her mother's side and to the royal court of Russia on her father's side. Born in the mid-1920s in North Staffordshire, England, she recalls having her first psychic experience at age two.

Her father, a second-generation White Russian, was among other things a Shakespearean actor, an astrologer, and a civil engineer. Sybil's mother, the lady of the house, was a native of southern Ireland.

In addition to her parents and her two sisters, Sybil grew up in a large household that included a great-grandmother, a grandmother, great-aunts, and aunts. The entire family, nineteen members at the time, regarded psychic phenomena as a normal process of life.

Although the future witch had read the classics at an early age, could recite the three R's without difficulty, and was casting youthful horoscopes in earnest, she received little formal education. Most of her tutelage came from her parents and relatives or a private tutor.

Later, though, at the age of twelve, Sybil's parents decided a formal educational experience would add to her training, and sent her off to a private English girls' school—a marked change from horoscopes, occult sciences, and herbology.

She attended the girls' school for three years, then returned home and subsequently met and fell in love with a man twenty-four years her senior. They eloped and were married when she was sixteen: he died just two years later, leaving her a young widow.

After the death of her husband, Sybil returned to her family. It was during this period that she was called upon to prepare for initiation into the witch's coven her Russian aunt presided over as high priestess—to replace a witch who had died. The witching ceremony took place in the South of France, where the coven existed and where the family traditionally wintered each year.

Following that winter season, the family returned to England and moved to a new home near the New Forest in Hampshire. The venturesome young Sybil soon became friends with a tribe of Gypsies nearby, and left home for two years to live with them in the New Forest.

By the time Sybil Leek was twenty-one, she had opened a successful antique shop in nearby Ringwood and later moved it to Burley, a small village in the heart of the New Forest. With a talent for writing, she also began authoring books and became a roving reporter for Southern TV.

Eventually her background as a witch led to the station doing a documentary film about her and witchcraft, which, in turn, was carried as a feature article in the Daily Herald, *an English newspaper. The ensuing publicity brought her an unexpected rash of calls and requests, as well as crowds of curiosity seekers about the shop and house. Sybil's second husband, Brian, soon became her only shield from the inquisitive public.*

Around the same time, a book she had written earlier about her career as an antique dealer, coupled with the widespread press coverage, prompted a call from New York, inviting her to appear on the "To Tell the Truth" show. The television appearance received wide media attention, formally introducing her to the American public.

After returning to England and suffering the death of her husband, she decided to give up her antique dealer business and pursue a new life and career in America with her family of two sons, Stephen and Julian.

Since settling in America, Mrs. Leek has spent her time professionally writing—her Diary of a Witch *has been a best seller—lecturing, making public appearances, researching, casting horoscopes (and not spells as far as anyone knows), philosophizing, and remaining faithful to her religion, witchcraft.*

PSYCHIC: What is a witch?
LEEK: A witch is a follower of *wicca*, or witchcraft, the ancient pre-Christian occult religion—the Old Religion. Contrary to most opinions, a witch is not anti-Christian and is not a heathen.

In America today the word "witch" is associated with Walt Disney or Salem and all the evil things one can think of. But in the greater part of Europe it must means what it is, a follower of witchcraft, whether male or female.

PSYCHIC: What do you think caused this "negative" connotation?
LEEK: Well, it started around the Middle Ages when witchcraft, which had been running side-by-side with the comparatively new religion of Christianity, was not just content to be a spiritual religion —its leaders began to take interest in material affairs, such as land. And many witches in the Middle Ages owned vast tracts of land.

If you'll trace this to the Salem days, you'll find that it's not so important that a group of girls had hysteria and the people became concerned, but the fact that Mrs. Nurse, one of the accused women, was also a very important landowner whose land bordered Governor Endicott's. That, I think, was the true reason for the Salem witch trials.

PSYCHIC: But that was some time ago.

LEEK: True, but the same thing will happen again and again. The real initiated witches, such as myself, not just the followers of witchcraft, are all highly successful. And people begin to ask why; they become suspicious and wonder how I earn such a good living, and I do.

Well, it isn't because I wave a magic wand or the fact that I have a belief in a religion, it's because I have within me a very good sense of timing. So, I don't make too many of the mistakes in business that perhaps other people would make. And my enthusiasm for a thing does not send me overboard. I wait until the timing is right, when the mechanism in me says *now*.

PSYCHIC: Why do you think witchcraft connotes antireligion in the West?

LEEK: Probably because of its secrecy and the little understanding about it. But witchcraft was forced into a secret organization; it went underground to survive. And yet the Christians, you know, had their own secret organization when they made the sign of the fish to note that they were meeting.

It's always a strange point as to which came first, magic or religion. I don't think there was any difference. Early man accepted magic and religion as being one; he didn't demand proof of it.

Now I accept the intangible without making demands upon it. But many people must have a figure of a God around their house; they must have something they can stretch their hands out and touch to strengthen their belief. I need nothing. I don't need an altar; I don't need anything to know that within the universe there is an intangible force that comes down to me, to you, and to all things living. Name it what you like—a Supreme Being or God—but it is there.

PSYCHIC: But why the secrecy in witchcraft?

LEEK: Because if you had lived for three hundred years with the threat of death around you—and don't forget, I have lived for two-thirds of my life with the idea that death could creep up on me by someone screaming witch—then the basic instinct becomes survival.

And witchcraft had to survive. It was driven underground by the impact of the new religion. So it took precautions to look after what it had got. In any religion, as with witchcraft, certain doctrines are secret and have been withheld from the public. These are the treasures; these are the things that had to be passed on to the next generation.

PSYCHIC: Yes, but how can witchcraft be understood if it remains a secret organization?

LEEK: Here I will go a little astray, because I do not believe that witchcraft is for everybody—as many people in our religion advocate. I do not discuss witchcraft in my life except when people ask me questions, and then I feel bound to answer with as much honesty as I can, according to my knowledge.

You cannot get everybody understanding the intangible any more than everyone could be a priest—whether a pagan priest or a Roman Catholic priest. And every religion has always had its inner religion, a religion for its people and a religion for its priests. You have the Kabbala in the Jewish religion and you have secrets in the Roman Catholic religion, which, incidentally, understands quite a lot about witchcraft. Nothing has ever been for everybody in religion.

PSYCHIC: It would appear that the Old Religion is in a dilemma, then, and that no one will ever understand it.

LEEK: But there is every reason to understand why the Old Religion has reached the stage of not being understood. First, it is not for everyone; second, it deals in intangibles; and third, it is effective in the realms of healing and understanding the mind.

Three hundred years ago you didn't go to a psychologist, you went to a witch, who understood the mind, which seemed to be magical. Going to the moon now seems magical for many. But thirty years ago if a child went to his father and said, "I'm going to be the first man on the moon," father would say to mother, "Don't you think we'd better take this boy to see a doctor?"

PSYCHIC: Well, then, what is witchcraft?

LEEK: Witchcraft is the Old Religion because it seems to go back to the time when man was first on earth, when he had those religious, spiritual feelings. I think it's a great mistake to think that man did not have religion until Christ and Buddha appeared.

It didn't just happen, it was inward, and we're going back to this as we go into the Aquarian Age [the astrological period of time, according to Mrs. Leek and other astrologers, we're cosmically entering]. Today more and more people are seeking the Deity within themselves, and this is a very healthy attitude; for if you don't find *It* within yourself, I doubt if you'll find *It* without.

And so we call witchcraft the Old Religion because this is a simple nature religion in which man, with no images, with nothing around him, has recognized that there was something greater than himself —some control and order in the world. For the sun rose and set and the planets moved in orderly procession; therefore, he felt he must be part of some sort of order, and we go back to the old laws of the universe—action and reaction, which today are also the basic laws of science.

PSYCHIC: What is the essence of the Old Religion, then?

LEEK: Basically, it is absolutely designed to be in tune with the components of the universe—male, female; positive, negative; action, reaction.

Our rituals are linked with the seasons—spring, summer, autumn, and winter—and we keep so very much to the universe. What we're really doing is giving a general hymn of praise to the universe and all the things in it. These are the ritualistic religious meetings, which the initiated witches will attend. But the followers of witchcraft might meet every two weeks or every four weeks, as they wish.

The quarterly meetings, then, are linked with the changes of the season, since the seasons are quite important to man in his own state of seeking harmony.

PSYCHIC: Don't these involve a certain number of people?

LEEK: Up to thirteen is a normal number for a coven of witches: six men and six women and a high priestess to act as both—above being male or female. She is the link between the rest of the people and the universe. She is the medium; "medium" means "between," you know. The high priestess becomes the medium between the universe and the people. And how strong she is will denote how well the meeting will go.

And I might add that *coven,* an old Anglo-Saxon word, simply means a meeting place, but with religion in mind.

PSYCHIC: Are you part of the priesthood of witchcraft?

LEEK: Yes, and not all can have the knowledge. My family does belong to the old priest and priestess cults; this is known. And it is up to us to continue and probably to increase the overall effect of the knowledge around people.

Now this may sound odd, but I don't believe in the equality of man. Today these are probably strange fighting words. I do not believe that everybody can be equal, because nobody's mind is equal. And that's why we believe absolutely in reincarnation. Everybody is not *ready* for the best things of life. Some people need the abrasive quality of living as part of their particular karmic path.

You see, in reincarnation you don't get the idea of retribution—hell, fire, and damnation—there's no punishment. The idea of sin varies in every age according to social environment, social conditions, and education. Sin has never been a constant thing. You could not say one thing is a sin forever and ever and ever in any religion, for it will vary.

PSYCHIC: What about the popular belief that your rituals involve unvirtuous ceremonies?

LEEK: You know, this is what amuses me. If all these things have been going on I feel a bit deprived. This is probably what it goes back to: one little word coming through and the connotation coming out badly.

Because witchcraft is a nature religion, the word "fertility" is used. This is not fertility of male and female. Male and female have always been able to keep up with their own fertility. But it was important at one time that the land and the cattle support human life. It was man's beseeching the Diety to help him survive with enough food, enough crops, to keep himself and his family. It was a very simple incantation

—that he and his family may live.

And this is basically what still occurs. We never incantate for money in our rituals. The invocation is for survival for mankind among the fruits of the earth, to be in his rightful place in the universe. That is the simple incantation which has been misconstrued into fertility rites. It's a very simple, stylized ceremony, with sounds and the trance and the elements of the four seasons as being important in your life.

And every invocation changes according to the season. The invocation in the spring has within it the means that the seed that is planted may grow; the invocation in August is that the harvest has been good and may we use it and divide it among us; and the invocation at Halloween is concerned that the long, dark winter may have within it the means for survival for you. It's a complete cycle of life, always acting and reacting.

PSYCHIC: Probably the most popularly known is Halloween; what is its significance in witchcraft?

LEEK: Halloween in America comes as a shock to me, because I never knew anything about trick or treat, until I came here. But to me, Halloween is our major religious festival, our new year. It's the new year of the Celtic world; to me a very religious celebration.

You see, Halloween is the time when we have the festival and the incantations concerned with renewing the psychic forces, when we ask for a renewal of strength within ourselves. It's the changeover, literally, from light to dark in the world—going into the dark period, almost like dying, and yet it is the beginning of a new year—and new life forces. This is the time of the rest period, so very necessary in the seasons; a time when the land lies fallow to be ready for the planting in the spring. And so you, as a human being, to a certain extent, lie fallow and are at your lowest ebb, but always ready with the spark of psychic awareness in you for when it is necessary.

PSYCHIC: Any goblins?

LEEK: Well, this is another thing I don't quite understand about Halloween in America. I never saw a goblin at any of my meetings. I'm not saying he wouldn't be welcome, though, if he came with love in his heart.

PSYCHIC: You talk about a "Deity"; what is It to you?
LEEK: This will probably sound sacrilegious, but I think we shall discover that It is not a mystical force, but an electrical one—a storehouse, which is linked by universal laws to all living things.
PSYCHIC: Is that your concept of God?
LEEK: I don't really like the word "God," because you can make a god out of a picture, out of a monkey-figure or even money. I want my Supreme Being to be so much greater than any of these things. I want It to be the ultimate, and It is, so far as I'm concerned.

Why do we want to make It into so many images? Even in the Christian religion battles go on among Baptists, Methodists, Roman Catholics—this worries me, because surely they are all part of one Deity.

So I believe there are dimensions, there are places which by the process of reincarnation we go up in a spiral toward a Central Force, a Universal Mind, a Deity. I don't believe there are Elysian fields, that we are a person on the other plane. I believe that we are a thought form, a vibration, a stream of energy, waiting, and then we change again into matter. I don't believe in God or the devil; as I have said, no hell, fire, and damnation.

PSYCHIC: What about white and black magic, then?
LEEK: If your intention is to destroy and to do evil, we consider that black magic. If your intention is to be constructive, then it is white magic. But the dominating force which engenders this is the same, make no mistake about that. This is the creative part of the universe coming out. It's seeking man's desire to be humane.

You see, the margin between white and black magic has always been very fine. Yet black magic has always been highly emphasized because the world is basically interested more in the evil than in the good. As far as religion goes, black magic does not have its own rituals. Being more destructive, it will take the ritual of another religion to degrade it. On the other hand, we have never taken the ritual of anybody else, we keep to our own. And I might add the greatest enemies to black magicians are white magicians, such as myself.

Now my main emphasis is this: let's not forget that black magic is in the world. Let's see it in perspective; don't let's see black magic as being *wicca,* meaning the Old Religion, because it isn't. It's an offshoot of it, just as the Spanish Inquisition, with all the terrible things that happened through it, was part of the Roman Catholic religion, but it is not truly the Roman Catholic religion.

So we must get things in perspective—that black magic is in the world and it's something that should not be encouraged any more than the Inquisition should be allowed to condemn the Catholic Church or be regarded in itself as a religion.

Persecution of different sects is not a good way to go through life harmoniously. Witchcraft struggles for harmony, and it starts in a selfish way. It starts by trying to put you, an individual, in a harmonious state.

PSYCHIC: For all of this, there doesn't seem to be much harmony between witchcraft and the religions of the world involving interaction, interchange.

LEEK: This is rapidly taking place, you'd be surprised, just as there's a bridge building between East and West in philosophy and religions. But I don't think witchcraft will be folded into this trend; I think it will always be unique, because it is involved with ancient wisdom and the constant search for truth. So many people are not able to face truth.

It will mean more people marching along the same road without throwing stones—a greater tolerance. I don't have to love or respect a person, but I do have to have tolerance. It used to be that perfect love casteth out fear, but now I believe perfect spirituality within yourself casteth out fear. I believe the deep spiritual feeling that one must have is the way to eliminate fear, because spirituality is beyond love. Love has a selfish element in it; spirituality doesn't.

PSYCHIC: You mention in your book, *Diary of a Witch*, an increase in the Old Religion and witches . . .

LEEK: Yes. And it is worldwide, not just here in America, which also has a lot of witches.

PSYCHIC: Why are so many, unlike you, unwilling to come out and say they are witches?

LEEK: Many of them will. But some of them don't have the oppor-

tunity that I do, by virtue of being other things in my life such as a writer, lecturer, astrologer. But the trend now is for many more people to talk, and one reason is that the witch laws have been repealed, practically all around the world.
PSYCHIC: Where must you still be cautious?
LEEK: Well, Mexico. Several years ago a witch was burned to death there.
PSYCHIC: What about the United States?
LEEK: I haven't gone through all the laws, though I believe that some states still have them. But it's not my fate to be arrested for witchcraft at all, I'm a liaison, a messenger.
PSYCHIC: Have you ever been persecuted for your beliefs and for being a witch?
LEEK: Oh, yes. But it doesn't bother me as it used to, when I was young, because I now understand the minds of the people who persecute. You see, man has a built-in mechanism for persecution. In phrenology it was called the organ of execution, which is really the organ of destruction. Man has as much a desire to destroy something as to create it.

And in my opinion, we have overemphasized this beautiful thing of creation. I think the thing that motivates destruction is fear, and fear is born through ignorance. So the effect of destruction of the victim isn't so important as *why* a person hates another sect.

But you were asking about persecution: there will always be persecution, the secret is *never* let it catch up to you, and to know yourself.
PSYCHIC: In your book you quoted your grandmother as saying, "Whatever you ardently desire, sincerely believe in, vividly imagine, and enthusiastically act upon, must inevitably come to pass." That sounds like something out of a personal dynamics course.
LEEK: I think a lot of people like Norman Vincent Peale picked up a few vibrations from my grandmother. And I'm not putting any restrictions on the good or evil results of this, either. You see, witchcraft is not a religion that is preaching that one thing is the only possible thing. Witchcraft makes allowances for the fact that man is not God

and, therefore, he has a proportion of good and evil in him. He is debilitated. The Deity can only be pure, which is the essence of truth and beauty and all that's good.

PSYCHIC: Then what, in your opinion, is man's role in all this?

LEEK: To realize that he is a part of a greater whole; to realize in his own individuality and personality that he is still only a bit of the universe, just a segment of a greater whole. The whole is a macrocosm and man is the microcosm—a lesser universe, but a universe in himself. I think he is striving toward an understanding of the universe of which he is a part. But I think he started trying to understand the universe instead of trying to understand himself first.

PSYCHIC: Is this part of your philosophy of reincarnation?

LEEK: Oh yes. And as we go into the new Aquarian Age, man is going back to saying, "I want to understand myself." If you understand that reincarnation is a progression toward perfection—perfection being contained in the greater whole—and if you understand that all the mistakes and miseries that come to you have a reason behind them, as they certainly have, then life becomes rather interesting to view.

It cannot be that some people were put into the world to have nothing and others seemingly to have everything. And it can't be that everybody came into the world with equal ideas. I'm not saying equal rights, either, because rights are something that man made for himself.

But reincarnation does become the link between the universe and man because it gives reasons why you will suffer at certain times and why you will be exhilarated at certain times. And it doesn't offer us the way so many other religions do, that you suffer because you are bad.

PSYCHIC: Then you must have your own ideas about the spirit of man.

LEEK: The spirit is the indestructible thing, we accept that. And we are beginning to see that it has an electrical force—a stream of energy —which is indestructible. I would describe the spirit as purified, apart from emotion, simply a force of energy, an electrical force, if you like.

PSYCHIC: How do you regard your psychic abilities?
LEEK: They're as much a part of me sitting here smoking a cigarette, or walking. I don't see them as supernatural. I see them as a highly developed part of me, no more than perhaps a great mathematician may be a super mathematician. He just carried out something that was originally there to a greater potential. This is what I have done.
PSYCHIC: Have you ever undergone any kind of tests by scientists to verify your psychic abilities?
LEEK: Everything, everything you can think of—sitting in electrical cages, sending thoughts through walls, all sorts of things.
PSYCHIC: Where?
LEEK: In Germany and in England, as well as in America. This has been going on, you know, since I was young. But you see I won't go through life being a guinea pig; this is my revolution. I'm revolting because I do all these trance sessions and it is part of my beautiful life going for somebody else. Six hours in a trance are six hours I could be enjoying music, or I could be being me. So it's reached the stage now where it has to be very scientific and directed toward some scientific experiment, and my time has to be paid for on the scale my writing is. And the experiment would have to be conducted efficiently with some status—not behind closed doors, anonymously, and not without the results known and public.

You see, we've got to get away from this amateurish way of thinking that the trance medium is at everyone's beck and call. You don't call in a scientist to tell him to drop everything because you want it proved that he can make a nuclear bomb. Things should be better arranged now, or else we're no better off than when I was a child.

Frankly, I don't give two hoots at this stage of my life about my psychic ability being validated; fame in the realm of psychic phenomena is nothing to me. I was a famous broadcaster, a famous playwright, and famous in music—so seeking fame has nothing to do with this.

Rather, the total recognition of psychic phenomena is what I would like to see—that no famous man is ashamed to be associated with it. And the man who dares be associated with it is the man who will be remembered.

I say the time has come now to put parapsychology on a really sound basis—at the universities. This is where it belongs.

PSYCHIC: What are some of the experiments you have participated in?

LEEK: Well, we filmed a table rising at the BBC studio in London; I was the first person of the BBC who ever did a program on psychic phenomena. The sound-recording man didn't like the idea, so he sat on the table and the next thing, his nose was on the wall—he was thrown off.

Then there was an experiment conducted at a haunted house in Old Southampton by an Oxford scientist, Professor Herbert. It was also filmed by the BBC. I also did a lot of psychometry with Professor Herbert. He would place packages on tables and ask me to name the contents. One time I got everything right, ten packages absolutely right. Another test he conducted with me was while I was in a moving car twenty-six miles away from him; I wrote down the message exactly transmitted through ESP, with a newspaperman, the driver, and two other people with me.

All of these experiments Professor Herbert filed with the Society for Physical Research in London. He was determined to file everything.

PSYCHIC: Do you have a "control" as some trance mediums do?

LEEK: No, but I may have. There might be a spirit around who helps me, perhaps my grandmother or somebody. But I don't call on any control. And I'm not a Spiritualist, definitely not a Spiritualist.

But the amazing thing now is I don't have to go into a deep trance. I can sit and see it, something apparently catalysts it off. Just what does, I don't know.

PSYCHIC: What do you think this phenomenon is?

LEEK: I think it means I'm very much in tune with a higher octave of the universe; I'm absolutely sure of this. And while I don't know which button is pushed, I know it happens.

PSYCHIC: You occasionally predict; have you ever registered your predictions with any scientific organizations?

LEEK: I have little to do with the scientific organizations, because I think they limit themselves. But make no mistake, I think they do good work.

PSYCHIC: Why not?

LEEK: Because many psychics like me are sick of being the Cinderellas of the world. Have you ever thought how it would be to pick up the phone and say, "Please, may I register a prediction with you?" Yet I'm not ashamed to put my name on any predictions or on any pieces of research. [True: In the January 1969 issue of *Playboy*, Mrs. Leek had gone on record there. She predicted that the Russians would be the first to land on the moon—in 1970—and that her main impression of the financial condition for the United States in 1969 would be one of a very depressed financial state, starting in February but reaching its climax in April—affecting many, many people.]

PSYCHIC: Is this why you call yourself the reluctant medium?

LEEK: Yes, because I don't care—except to know why there are people like myself. Everybody thinks I should care and put this thing foremost in my life. I only see it as a facet of my life. Besides, it's distasteful to find in America the amount of charlatans that are literally feasting on the thing that I regard as a very precious but natural thing of my life. The need is there for a psychic and there are not enough to go around, so you get the cheap little charlatan cashing in. And I do not believe that you can turn on your psychic splendor, if you like, every fifteen minutes for appointments.

Actually, the best way for seeing psychic phenomena is without all this terrible veil of mysticism—when you don't have to put on a gramophone record with a hymn before you can get into a room to have a séance. In short, the time has come when we don't have to dress psychic awareness up in the guise of being a religion. It is *not* a religion. We don't have to dress it up as being anything more than what it is—a part of you, or at least of some people.

PSYCHIC: In *Diary of a Witch* (page 16), you state that you see little difference in magic and science, except that magic is one step ahead. That's a rather bold statement.

LEEK: I know, but science is so slow—isn't it really? This is why it's important for science not to despise magic, and magic not to despise science. The church made the big mistake all the way through, always against science. What is there to lose by cooperation?

Science and occultism deal in the same things—intangibles. It's intangible until somebody pulls it out of the air; then it's tangible. Now the atom was always there, wasn't it?

PSYCHIC: Then you think psychic phenomena themselves can become tangibles?

LEEK: Yes, if allied with science there will be a perfectly rational explanation. And whenever highly developed people like myself are allied with science, inasmuch as we have certain centers that are open to awareness—extra eyes, extra senses, not only a sixth sense, but more awareness—this will become a part of the structure of the body to be able to check up on. You know, like, "Have you had your psychic checkup this month?"

PSYCHIC: You also state in your book that "the witch's interest in magic causes her to investigate the laws of nature." How so?

LEEK: The laws of nature are the laws of the universe, positive and negative, inasmuch as a seed will grow into a plant or a flower, will reach maturity, and then return to the soil, therefore changing the force of energy, the force of life into a piece of matter again. This all seems again to link to something of the magic of reincarnation in a very practical manner.

The witch is as interested in science as the scientist is, because the scientist must ultimately go back to the basic laws of the universe, which the witch's religion is founded on—the laws of action and reaction.

And whether scientists like it or not, whether occultists like it or not, science and occultism are gradually going to get together until they are working in parallel. That's when we'll get some advances.

PSYCHIC: Is this what you advocate?

LEEK: Yes. I want some parapsychologist, somebody, before I die, to tell me why there are people like myself. As I grow older I think I'm getting nearer to understanding this, but it has nothing to do with the accepted things of mysticism. You see, I reject mysticism and this makes it very complicated for people to understand.

And I do not think what I have is a gift from God; equally so, I don't think it's a gift from the devil—as my enemies would like to say. But I do believe that I have a peculiar metabolism, something happens, which causes these phenomena. It's like setting a computer into action, only I am the computer.

PSYCHIC: Do you think psychedelic drugs have a place in all this?

LEEK: I have a great curiosity about hallucinogenic drugs because this again is part of the theme: people searching. The drugs have a place, but unfortunately the wrong people use them—those who are not ready for them. I don't think you can hop, skip, and jump through different incarnations. We *need* this process of learning and experiencing and doing things. And drugs don't give us that opportunity. Although I do not condemn the use of drugs, I dislike their misuse. We got them too soon.

On the other hand a person like Aldous Huxley profited by drugs because he already had a lot going for him; he wasn't trying to escape from living. Now if you're going to use drugs as an escape route, then you're going to be nothing.

I also know that drugs have been used in many religious ceremonies and in many ritualistic practices. There's a place in religion for drugs, not only in pagan religions, but in many orthodox religions.

But the thing is, when the Indian decides to take peyote, he's prepared for it. He doesn't take it as a kick to escape life, because he knows he will never get any benefit from it. He prepares himself with seven days of religious fasting and duties. Preparation is the secret.

But there are other means of extending one's harmony with the universe; drugs are not the real answer. The answer is in accepting reincarnation and the idea of spiritual development. This is how you really get the best out of living—we get back to man's awareness and his place in the universe.

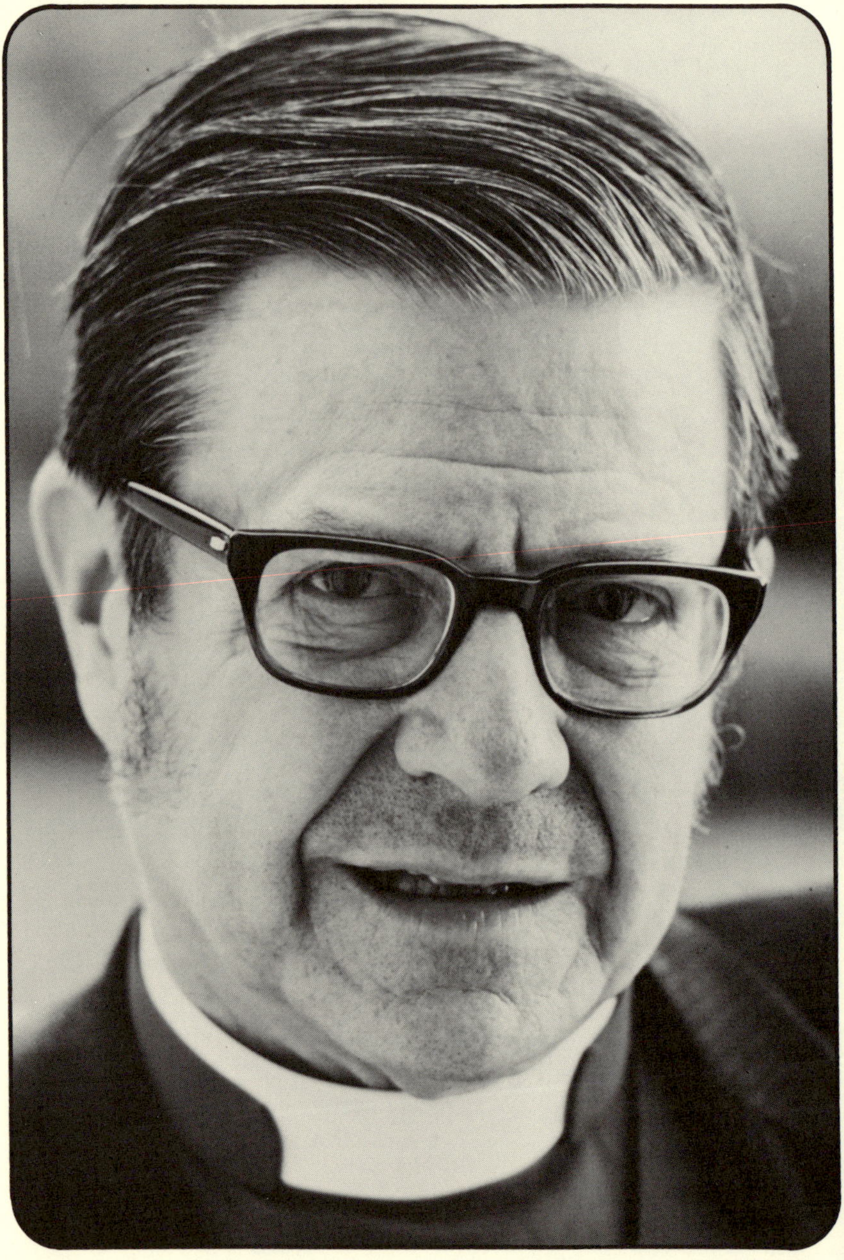

nine
James A. Pike

James Albert Pike was born in Oklahoma City on St. Valentine's Day, 1913. His parents, James and Pearl Pike, both natives of Kentucky, had established the family home in the Sooner State's capital city shortly before, where his father owned a typewriter sales agency and his mother taught high school.

The unexpected early death of his father in 1915, however, abruptly changed the family's plans. Five years later, to take advantage of greater opportunites in California's school system, his mother moved their home to Hollywood. Jim, an only child, was seven at the time.

A Roman Catholic during those formative years—having inherited the religion from his parents—James Pike attended both public and parochial schools. It was at St. John's Military Academy in Los

Angeles, a junior high school operated by the Sisters of Mercy, that he began to display academic and leadership abilities, rising to staff officer of the student battalion and editor of the Academy's paper, Bugle Call.

Later at Hollywood High School, he served as assistant editor of the yearbook, won the school's scholastic debating-team contest, as well as the Los Angeles citywide competition and graduated first in his class.

From high school, young Pike entered the Jesuit University in Santa Clara, California, with thoughts of preparing for the priesthood, but two years later transferred to the University of California at Los Angeles to study law—though not before winning the Catholic university's debating contest and the intercollegiate competition.

After graduating from U.C.L.A. in 1936 with degrees in both Law and the Arts and having served as editor of the school's paper, The Daily Bruin, the young attorney went on to Yale, where he was awarded a Doctor of Science of Law degree at the age of twenty-six. That was in 1938, the same year he and a girl he had known from Hollywood were married. Unsuccessful, though, the marriage ended two years later.

By the time World War II had erupted, James Pike had served as an attorney with the Security and Exchange Commission in Washington, had become a member of the bar of the U.S. Supreme Court, and had taught law classes at George Washington University. He also admitted at the time to an agnostic outlook toward religion, although as he has stated, "I wasn't anti-church, I just dropped out."

It was also in Washington, in 1942, that he met and married Esther Yanovsky, the mother of his four children—Catherine, James Jr. (who preceded him in death), Constance, and Christopher. The marriage ended in divorce in the mid-1960s.

James Pike's war years were spent mostly as a naval intelligence officer and later as an attorney for the Maritime Commission and the War Shipping Administration. While still in uniform, the call to *religion re-entered his life and he joined the Episcopal Church. In 1944 Dr. Pike was ordained a deacon and subsequently made a curate.*

After the war and with religion his focal point, the future bishop entered formal religious studies at the Virginia Theological Seminary, later transferring to Union Theological Seminary in New York, where he was awarded a Bachelor of Divinity degree, magna cum laude. He was ordained to the priesthood in 1946.

Bishop Pike's rise to Fifth Episcopal Bishop of California in 1958 was swift and punctuated with other prominent church positions, including chaplain of Columbia University, chairman of Columbia's Department of Religion, and dean of St. John the Divine in New York City, largest Protestant church and cathedral in the world. From the 1950s on, Pike became known for his liberal positions on most of the great social issues, including McCarthyism, birth control, censorship, war and peace, civil rights, etc.

His subsequent questioning of certain church dogmas, which led to an attempt, later dropped, to try him for heresy, is now legend, as was his final decision to leave the church.

A prolific writer, James Pike authored many books and articles on law, religion, and ethics. Books have included You and the New Morality, A Time for Christian Candor, What Is This Treasure?, If This Be Heresy, *and* The Other Side.

In addition to serving as a member of the U.S. Food for Peace Council and acting as Chairman of the California Advisory Committee to the U.S. Commission on Civil Rights, James Pike was awarded a dozen honorary doctorates and awards, one of which was the Medallion of Valor from the State of Israel.

Before his death in the Israeli desert in September, 1969, he and his wife, Diane, and a group of clergymen founded the Foundation for Religious Transition.

PSYCHIC: Why do you think your questioning of certain religious church dogma along with your active open interest in psychic phenomena have upset so many people?

PIKE: I think people who are fairly conventional or orthodox in the Christian religion become threatened by psychic phenomena because the subject challenges their own beliefs, such as the confrontation of Jesus as a man as opposed to the God-tradition of Easter.

That is, they regard this set of psychic phenomena of the Easter tradition—the death of Jesus and His ongoing . . . with His disciples—as sheer miracle, having nothing to do with the nature of man as man, which to me seems paradoxical.

Perhaps they should pay heed to a very important thing from St. Paul, First Corinthians, chapter fifteen, in which he says with regard to these phenomena: "If all men don't rise after death"—that is, go on—" then Jesus didn't either." To me, if Jesus didn't rise we have no message.

St. Paul further says, "But some men will ask how are the dead be raised up, with what kind of body do they come?" Notice the question is generic, it's not, How did Jesus rise? And he caps it with, "Flesh and blood do not inherit—they do not go on." In other words, it is not a physical body, it is a *pneumatikon soma*—airy, etheric, if you wish.

The important point here is that by talking about Easter, we've been affirming the psychic field all along.

Then I find the liberal Christians threatened by the explanation of Jesus' survival. It's challenging because a lot of them hadn't believed this, anyway. Therefore, when you show them some data about survival and say, "How about the data reported about Jesus?" Well, now to them that has to be faith.

PSYCHIC: Is your interest in psychic phenomena an outgrowth of inherent inquisitiveness or belief, does it stem from your legal and clergy background, or is it entirely a result of the experience following your son's death?

PIKE: Both, rather than either/or. But I feel that categories you mention here are rather insightful. You sort of dig me, because the first ones are how I respond to any sort of new experiences. I'm never content to have a new experience happen and not try to grasp it or take it in without some kind of mental or intellectual frame of reference.

Hence, when the experiences after my son's death happened, I felt it necessary to pursue what seemed to be attention-getting phenomena. This led me to seek a medium, a professional in this field, recommended by Canon John S. Pierce Higgins, vice provost of the Southern Cathedral in England. Her name was Mrs. Ena Twigg.

I also felt the need then to read, study, and consult the scientific minds in the field. Having been a lawyer and also a naval intelligence officer, I'm kind of an investigator in the sense that I'm trained a little bit to distinguish fact from fancy and fact from theory. I say that nonpejoratively about theory.

PSYCHIC: Then psychic phenomena were something that naturally came along for you?

PIKE: Right. I probably never would have been stimulated had there not been direct experiences. I really can't imagine myself starting out to explore this field, because I have so many other things central to me, like Christian origins, social action and concern, civil rights, war and peace; I'm too busy to have taken on another field.

For example, there may be something to astrology, but if you asked me three years ago, I would have said, "Absolutely not." But having read enough now of C. G. Jung and his theory on synchronicity of things in the universe, and having begun to develop a general field theory about all this sort of psychic field, I'm not now prepared to say there isn't anything to astrology. As a matter of fact, I have kind of a hunch maybe there is. But I'm not about to go off and study astrology, unless of course, something happens in my life which is very striking astrologically.

PSYCHIC: Psychic phenomena cover a broad range; what in particular interests you?

PIKE: I'm interested in what you might call a general field theory for all these phenomena—what they mean for the here and now, without in the least minimizing what they might mean for continuity and survival.

I now think there's a relationship with all facets of life, a larger unity that we don't fully grasp, and that ordinary methods of measurement and ordinary limitations are transcended. Perhaps this can be all tied together in terms of what we can learn about better interpersonal relations, because if we can understand whatever is going on in any area, we can better use it and certainly it has some bearing on life.

PSYCHIC: Have you looked into peripheral subject matter with which this field is often popularly associated, such as palmistry, numerology, and other so-called mystic sciences?

PIKE: No, I haven't, although my daughter Connie had her palm read by a Samaritan priest when we were visiting the Holy Land. I must admit he was clicking it off pretty well and I was quite impressed.

But getting back to what I call a general field theory. If there's something to the synchronicity concept of the late Dr. Jung, if there's something to the collective unconscious, if there's something to a universe in which everything is involved and tied together, and if time and space are limiting concepts only to our conscious minds and maybe not to reality as such—then certainly there is room left for things like palmistry, numerology, astrology.

Without special study I'm not capable of verifying anything about any of these, but I don't have the "no" to them that I did previously, which is something of a gain I think.

PSYCHIC: Why did you write the book, *The Other Side*?

PIKE: Several reasons. I felt enough had happened here and that I should write it up; I had a commitment to a publisher on two other books, which I traded for writing this one; and the news, including the total picture, that came out of the Toronto séance with Arthur Ford had become somewhat confused.

In addition, I felt that the credibility in this kind of field depends on putting all the evidence, or at least a great deal of it, down clearly and analytically—as opposed to the scattered press reports. The reporting I'm not complaining about too much, considering the limited space reporters and headline writers must work in. But to me that which was coming across was confusing and I was appearing to be a rather gullible person. So I put it ahead in priority of other tasks because I felt there was a need to hear about the "other side" in the two meanings I used the phrase: the other side of credulity and the other side of death.

It was my wife, Diane, by the way, who organized the material and kept the book going, because my attempts to write it were not working out too well. I was plugging away at it haphazardly, and it was becoming emotionally difficult, as well. That's how it became possible to get it out.

And I might add that it was very therapeutic, kind of a freeing-up process. Working it all through as honestly as I knew how externalized everything and put it in a much clearer and understandable perspective—something like good analysis would do.

PSYCHIC: A critical comment that has been raised is how you could sell your son's grief.

PIKE: Well, I've not heard it put just that way, but I've heard the phrase, "You have used your son," and so forth. I suppose one could amplify on that and say, How could he sell his son's grief, his own grief, and that of others?

I weighed that pretty carefully and saw on reflection no way in which publishing this would be harmful at all. And certainly I didn't feel Jim's reputation would suffer because of what people might think —the kind of people I respect who look at things nonjudgmentally. In fact I was confident that it would be aided somewhat if people knew the background and what came through afterward.

PSYCHIC: What about Jim, himself?

PIKE: I had received no negative from him about this. Now I want to be very careful here, because I did not attach too much weight to that as such. I only state it as the absence of a negative.

How much of that could be my own unconscious, subconscious mind playing out through the medium as the record, and how much of that could be the enthusiasm of the medium—who after all is professionally involved in this field and who thinks the more people write it up, the better—is unknown.

And if it were Jim saying this, as I stress in the book, anything coming through from him is not coming as from an oracle. He's not infallible, nor does he have unlimited knowledge. If that were his opinion it still doesn't mean it's the best thing to do.

PSYCHIC: That's certainly an interesting and important point, the fallibility.

PIKE: A very important point, I think. I find some people engaged in a lot of overbelief here. They think that a message from the other side —considering the nature of how it comes—makes it true. Well, it would be rather naïve, I think, just automatically to believe it.

Maybe it's good advice and certainly you ought to take it seriously, but I don't think it's infallible—because even if the person were alive you wouldn't do everything or believe everything he told you.

So I mention that only to say to those who say, "Well, you've used your son," perhaps he was using me. That's at least the way it was coming through.

PSYCHIC: What kind of general response did you receive from the book?

PIKE: For one thing, I have been reassured about the difficult decision to do it, which certainly vindicated, "How could he?"

I've never been involved in anything where mail was so favorable —about forty to one on the positive side. And we tried to answer all of it, whether for or against, except the psychoceramic or crackpot type.

A large response came from parents in terms of how do you keep some influence in there and at the same time not seem to be authoritarian, without driving the young people away and out of the house. Young people at Jim's age level found the book quite helpful, too. Response also indicated that it personally helped and carried a great deal of significance for people in bereavement.

On the other hand, fundamentalist Christians told me that what I experienced, as reported in the book, was the work of the devil and his henchmen.

In addition, we didn't have much mail from the clergy, except the fundamentalist type, which is very interesting. One would expect some kind of marked positive response from the clerics, considering our teaching about life everlasting.

PSYCHIC: Did you attempt any additional contacts with your son after you wrote the book?

PIKE: Very little. There was one with Mrs. Twigg, which was added as a postscript in the book. That was when my daughter Connie, Diane, her brother, and I were in England—I was returning from Jerusalem after the book was completed and for no special reason decided to visit the medium. We recorded the session, but felt it would be too late to add to the book, although it was sent to the publisher anyway. As I mentioned, the publisher added it as a postscript.

There was only one other time. My son Chris, Jim's younger brother, had visited me and discovered in the guest room, where he always stayed, an old alarm clock which had stopped at 8:19. Well, this was a couple of days after another poltergeist-type phenomenon involving some pills had occurred—they had been placed in an old shaving kit of mine and not by me.

Now this to me, operationally and pragmatically, is exactly the same as if I had been away and I found a note on my desk from my secretary to call someone.

I take it as an attention-getting or notice-giving device. So, I ended up calling George Daisley [the medium in Santa Barbara mentioned in *The Other Side*] and made an appointment. It was not a remarkable session, in that a number of things seemed to be relevant but nothing extraordinary occurred. That's been the only other time.

PSYCHIC: Have you formed any new hypothesis about whether you did or didn't communicate with your son since you wrote the book?

PIKE: No. In the last chapter we spelled out the alternatives as fully as we knew how. I still leave it there and, with the first alternative

—survival—as being the easier for me to believe, the more plausible.

But that's the most I can say: that it is the most plausible hypothesis in the light of the whole context—I *believe* it, but I don't *know* it. It never happened to me before and it never has again.

However, there is a third one that I am beginning to notice: the concept of possession. For example, in cases of reincarnation, when a person thinks he's recalling certain things from past lives, he is perhaps being possessed by the deceased person. I haven't really given any thought to that, other than to see on the horizon the possibility for some of the phenomena.

PSYCHIC: Have you any definite opinion now about what life after death holds for an individual? How does this differ at all from your earlier convictions?

PIKE: In January, before my son died, I had stated publicly at a theological college in Cambridge, while wearing the purple rabat and clerical collar, that after my process of facts plus faith—testing out everything empirically—I had concluded that there weren't enough facts on which to base the affirmation of survival or life after death.

Up to very near that point, I would have affirmed continuity of personality beyond death—in a possibility of growth or decline. I affirm freedom to chose at points here and hereafter, with no fixed heaven or hell except as one would see these as images of peace or misery, where you would be or can be right now.

But then I decided I didn't affirm this any more and I didn't need to, because here is where we are and this is where we're called to be, to serve in joy and to rejoice—the one-world-at-a-time thing. If there is more, okay, we'll cope with it when we get there.

PSYCHIC: In effect, the psychic phenomena gave you new data to revise your opinion.

PIKE: Right. The events which occurred and the séances restored my belief in survival. But I had not yet read enough to think of the other alternatives we have discussed, either—ones that would not require a personal survival hypothesis.

Also interesting is the literature in this field coming from other people who have analyzed data and who come out with the same view on survival that I held before—without psychic phenomena—which happens to be very congenial with my Anglican heritage.

Also, Anglican theology had tended to be universalistic, believing that all men in due time will have made it in the life to come by free choice. As St. Paul says, "God would be all in all."

Now this is contrary to orthodox theology and its eternal hell. Yet it had not been characteristic of Anglicans, anyway. So oddly enough, it all seems to fit together. And this is my view of it—of life after death.

PSYCHIC: A much more democratic process instead of an either/or.

PIKE: In a sense, yes. Now, reincarnation in my mind is not contradictory, either. It would simply be a mode through which this could be worked out. That is, that you might choose, and it seems to be choice, to re-enter the "physical" mode.

PSYCHIC: Is reincarnation inconsistent with Christianity?

PIKE: That's a different question from, "Is it true?" However, I don't see anything contrary to the general Judaic-Christian tradition. Four out of eight of the early church fathers—there were four Latin and four Greek—believed in reincarnation. That's a pretty good percentage.

The Samaritans believed that their Restorer would be the new Moses or Moses come back. And the Fourth Gospel sounds like that's what Jesus is, because He did everything Moses did—a physical return, if you will.

And what else could the Second Coming doctrine mean, which not many Christians believe any more? If He comes back that's certainly reincarnation.

That's what astonishes me about the orthodox biblical people. It's easier for me to say that I'm impressed with Dr. Stevenson's reincarnation data and research than it is for them. I should think they would embrace Stevenson as a friend, but they don't. They're the ones most horrified.

PSYCHIC: How does your view of the material world fit into your philosophy of ongoing life or life after death?

PIKE: I have the feeling more and more it's all one unity. And I'm less sure about words like "material" or "spiritual"; I don't quite know what they mean, any more.

I would say if we mean this span of life that we know more about and which seems to end in a process known as death, I am very enthusiastic about it, enthusiastic about making it as decent a place as possible. I think it's our calling, because it's where we are.

To me, everything is moving along together. Each of us is a part of what can be, not only in terms of our own fulfillment, but in the terms of others, who are separate—one from each other.

I guess "forever" is a safe enough word in terms of what the total possibilities are for everything, because I know of no basis for putting a terminus to reality.

PSYCHIC: What, then, do you think is the purpose of life?

PIKE: The purpose of life, now and hereafter, would seem to me to try to become more one's self—greater openness, sensitivity, awareness, capacity to love others, and so forth. I think to be one's true self is the ultimate dimension, more interconnection and continuity with the One or the All.

And as this happens, one has more and more joy, effectiveness, and service for others. This is the purpose of it all. It's a dynamic, a more and more kind of feeling.

PSYCHIC: That has a familiar philosophical ring to it.

PIKE: Well, I've gone pretty Hindu-Buddhist on this. But I think it's a question of enlightenment of what and who you are, rather than "salvation," which means having the wrath of God worked off by grace some way.

I think less in those terms and more in terms that *I am* God, just as you and everybody else are, too. I don't really know it yet, I mean in terms of the way I totally function. If I did, then I'd be able to say who I am. But that would mean nothing arrogant, because I say that everyone else is, too.

PSYCHIC: Why do you think psychic subject matter has become so popular?

PIKE: I think it represents what has already happened to our culture in principle and practice: *the triumph of the empirical method.*

And the mystical experience somehow represents the hope of making direct contact with ultimate reality, whether through transcedent cosmic consciousness or psychedelic experiences—with or without drugs. Apparently there are a variety of ways to the mystical or what it represents.

And I'm very impressed with the nondrug type of psychedelic experience that's being developed at the University of California Medical School, which I mentioned in the book.

Also, I think the churches are rapidly declining because they haven't caught on yet—particularly the respectable ones, which kind of protect members from any such mystical happenings. Can you imagine in an Episcopal church, a bishop sitting there and laying on hands, two by two, if anybody started speaking in tongues or anything? Why, he would probably make a psychiatric referral or it would make him lose his lines! In other words, we don't really expect any direct experience to happen.

So I think this mystical quest or desire to make direct contact with ultimate reality—which is an old one and which is what religion is all about—is very much connected with this interest.

I think it's man's capacity—his psychic or psi capacity—to try to transcend space and time even now. There's no reason it shouldn't be after death because that transcends the limitations of this corpus.

And I think survival is part of that larger here and now capacity man has. If he doesn't have it now, he's not going to have it then —if I don't have now that which survives, I'm not going to survive.

Also, I don't accept the more standard Christian view that God gives a kind of special gift to the elect, conferring resurrection on them.

Either it's natural or it's nothing. So it's true for everybody, you see.

Now the Fourth Gospel approach is pretty good, saying that we are even now in eternal life, and that's how I would put it. So I would say that this segment of eternal life is as important as any other I'm going to be in, so why should I have my mind just on heaven?

PSYCHIC: Such a premise as eternal life would presume we antedated what we are, wouldn't it?

PIKE: Well, it could assume the reincarnation theory or mean that a new being could come that henceforth will survive. Either one is quite possible.

I try to avoid the word "eternal" out of empirical considerations because I have seen no survival evidence which establishes or verifies that anything is eternal, although I use the word when reciting the Fourth Gospel, St. John—as quoted here. "Survival" is a much safer word.

Perhaps, though, eternal life could be taken somewhat mythologically or poetically to mean "life of a certain quality," which I think we have, that transcends what is time-bound and space-bound.

Yet I don't see any reason it should not be eternal; I'm not putting any terminus on it.

PSYCHIC: It seems that even science is becoming a little more tolerant, while the new science of parapsychology is experiencing more popularity. Do you think this is a result of a more sympathetic public opinion or that dogmatic disciplines and institutions are reassessing their own structures, thus becoming more open-minded to the possibility of other dimensions and more unknown natural laws and forces?

PIKE: If you take the question mark off that question, I'll gladly adopt it as a statement. It's exactly what's happening, I think, among other things we've discussed.

For example, psychology itself was once regarded as the bunk—and even the psychiatry, within medicine, was pure superstition, which has been the story of new disciplines.

But scientists are very reticent these days to say something can't be. They might devote a lot of time to saying what you claimed, wasn't. But that's different from saying it can't be.

PSYCHIC: Do you see any common denominator to the dissent of some of the youth, the present decline of religion, and the growing use of drugs, along with new convictions about material goods?

PIKE: Yes, I see a connection between all of this. First, there has been a considerable disappointment, disenchantment with their father's and mother's generation, and not necessarily enthusiasm about their own, either.

Then, a lot of young people have been put off by the Vietnam war, as well as the inability to do anything about the cities and the awful condition of minority groups. All this kind of piled up and caused them to challenge authority, and with this the whole bag of values turns gray for them.

They also question what would cause somebody to suffer heart attacks and strokes merely to obtain three chrome-plated cars, a big swimming pool and house, and belong to exclusive, discriminating clubs.

So perhaps they feel there must be more than that, and this turns them to the religious quest, which through desiring a short-cut brings them to the psychedelic drug route.

PSYCHIC: How do you regard this route?

PIKE: Harsh and dangerous—I know from my son's experience. But you see, these young people are still using a lot of the methods and ways of the generation they reject, such as doing things in a hurry. You could call LSD instant Zen. Most of them don't want to go off on a long retreat and meditate for months; they want it to happen tonight.

This is just part of the scene, along with the principle of authority. When authority becomes a question, they think about it, and finally there is no authority that is final to them.

But more important is the respect given to individuals for how sound and truthful they are, rather than accepting something as true merely because it comes from leaders or authorities. It's just the reverse, you see. Accepting a person for what he is—his ethics and truthfulness—not his position, which is applying more and more to many people.

PSYCHIC: Would you say that the common denominator is antihypocrisy?

PIKE: No. I think hypocrisy is just one of the things that shows up so noticeably in a time of transition like this. The common denominator, I think, is the triumph of the empirical method—looking at it the way it is, saying it the way it is.

Yet, they're capable of their own biases, too. If they're put off by something they'll reject the whole category. A student once said to me very hostilely, "Why do you go on saying that people roast in hell forever?" and I said, "Well, I don't say that." And he said, "You've got to; you're supposed to." To which I answered, "But I don't have to say it." You see he had rejected me because he associated me with established religion.

PSYCHIC: Do you think man is developing a greater awareness of the universe and his meaning to it?

PIKE: Some are, and I feel that the best of youth is getting nearer to what the real question is. I think there's a greater respect for all the values we're talking about here.

Just take the difference in the kind of ethical norm. There is now respect for some people who don't do what they're told, you see. Also, there is this "saying it the way it is" thing.

In this regard, my own children can be frank to the point of being painful. But in general, that's pretty good compared with the proprieties of saying just what father wants them to say.

There's a certain honesty that's respected, too, making heroes out of some of the people society classifies as criminals. Father Dan Berrigan, Father Philip Berrigan, Father Tom Melville, and others of the Catonsville Nine who used napalm on papers not on babies. These are heroes to my kids, not the people prosecuting them.

All this I think is a greater sensitivity toward interpersonal relationships—the personal, the loving, the courageous. To the freed-up people it says: "I will go to prison before I will violate my conscience." And that was not a good idea before, you see.

The ideals have changed. Who are the bad guys; who are the good guys?

PSYCHIC: What kind of reading do you get from this?

PIKE: Well, to me it is the basis for a *really* mature basis for decision. I think there's also a lot less judgmentalism about other people's behavior. And we're less and less speaking to the people saying, "You've got to do this or that." More and more we're saying, "Here are the options." Now that's mature and healthy.

PSYCHIC: Have you ever experimented with psychedelic drugs?

PIKE: No. I've studied enough, talked to enough people, and early enough began to see their destructive effects on my own son, that I'm not particularly eager to.

On the other hand, I'm not really opposed to psychedelic drugs, since I am aware of their sensible scientific uses.

An alcoholic clinic in Baltimore makes use of them in alcoholic recovery. Then certain types of psychoanalysis make use of them, plus my research in religious origins confirms that almost every religion has in its earlier stages used psychedelic drugs corporately for the principal sacrament.

PSYCHIC: Do you think that some people in this country might be leaning toward the Eastern philosophies because they are more open to mystical experiences?

PIKE: I would say so. Mystical experience has been a phenomenon found among the adherents of every religion. But in general the Western religions or religions of the book—Christianity, Judaism, Islam—have often looked on it with grave suspicion.

The Eastern religions, on the other hand, have encouraged mystical experiences. They have an ontology, cosmology, a metaphysic in which this fits better—the unit of experience or sense of continuity with the All, the One, the Divine.

This fits the theology better than Western religions, where there is a gap between the infinite and the finite, separating the Creator and the creature, causing a dichotomy.

The Eastern thing, therefore, is fitting more into this quest, giving a sense of communion. Unlike Western religions, Eastern religions have never made the claim of exclusiveness. In fact, they're like blotting paper in absorbing any kind of religious claims made by anybody, which further exemplifies the communion.

PSYCHIC: With all the factions for change in our country, where do you think we're headed?

PIKE: I think the old structures and values are nearing their end, while a lot of green shoots are growing up at the same time. The question is whether the new will come fast enough to give meaning and hold society together. To me, it's like one house collapsing and within it a new one going up. The question is whether we can get the roof of this new house up in time to keep the rain out—or nuclear fallout, if you wish—as the other collapses.

We're in a transition, and the public is remarkably numb to some of the very big things that could be the end of us. Population explosion, air pollution, water pollution, and so on, get little concern.

But I'm basically very optimistic that somehow if we just keep talking about it and educating, maybe we'll find the way.

PSYCHIC: Would you say that because of all this your general approach and outlook on life have changed considerably in the past few years?

PIKE: Very much so, on all realms of life. Life-style and what is important to people, what heals people, a great deal more openness, much less uptightness, much more experimental and empirical toward life, almost all judgmentalism disappears. For instance, this whole psi field has opened up a much bigger view of human potential for me. The potential of interrelationship, the sensitivity of the mystery of all that goes on between persons beyond just their words or their actions or touches. There are things like AM and FM and everything else going on, and we're just beginning to discover some of this. Therefore, the wonder of each other person and the greater awareness of the beauty found in the other person is true of everyone.

And I've found that if you can somehow let yourself be open, there is something exciting to be found, something warm to be loved, to be received, which I think is connected with the whole psi field very much.

The idea that there are more lines of connections in this universe than I ever realized, that we're sending and receiving more signals, is a key. I put ESP, psychic phenomena, the things that point toward survival, and so on in the same bag.

Somehow all are connected to a collective unconscious and a kind of panentheistic world-view. And it then becomes a much grander kind of world, more exciting where every experience is a joy. To me this is all renewing—I feel I'm growing younger.